ANNA & ANDERS JEPPSSON

SIMPLE AND STYLISH
backyard projects

Preface

Figuring out new woodworking projects and tackling practical problems can be a lot of fun. I find it interesting and creative to sit and sketch how I want things to look and what purpose they should serve. Most often, the need to make new things is mine, then a new product will evolve, based on my frequently illegible sketches and explanations— , and Anders' ability to decipher them.

When spring arrives, we constantly have new needs and wishes for items to complete the garden or the terrace. And building them is always a pure pleasure for Anders. He loves watching how a pile of lumber transforms into a table, a bench or some other useful item. And I love it when the product is finished and I can give him the next interesting challenge!

It is especially fun to make things for the garden. The finish need not be as perfect as for indoor items, and if you bring a crosscut saw, miter saw, a screwdriver and some other tools on the patio you might end up having a really good time. My job is to bring out the camera to immortalize the projects in the afternoon sun on a warm August day. All I can say is: I have the best job in the world!

In this book we present projects built for our garden and patio, but we have also tackled the needs and requests of a number of our friends and acquaintances. You can either follow the drawings in the book to the letter, or you can treat the projects as ideas to inspire you, and build according to your own design. You will notice that most of our projects are made of pine painted white. This is simply because we like it and it suits our home. As you read through the book, take an extra look at the pictures and ask yourself: What preferences do I have? What colors or types of wood fit in my home? Should I try different measurements? Let your inspiration flow!

Here's wishing you a long, warm and wonderful summer!

Anna Jeppsson

Contents

Welcome to the Garden

This sign on the way into our garden is like a three-dimensional picture. Since we are knick-knack crazy, we always bring more or less "unnecessary" things home from our travels. Here, we found a use for a clock and gecko from Portugal, and the Greek goddess Aphrodite finally found her home on the shelf. The sign looks welcoming and original, at least that's what our guests think.

Materials

Tongue-in-groove board, $^3/_4 \times 3^3/_4$ inches,
approx. 9 feet 10 inches:
    5 pieces × 23$^5/_8$ inches (A)
Chair Rail Moulding, $^5/_8 \times 2^3/_4$ inches,
approx. 39 inches:
    2 pieces × 15$^3/_4$ inches (B)
Planed strip, $^1/_4 \times 1^3/_4$ inches, approx. 59 inches:
    2 pieces × 18$^1/_8$ inches (C)
    2 pieces × 10$^1/_4$ inches (G)
Planed strip, $^1/_2 \times ^1/_2$ inches, approx. 23$^1/_2$ inches:
    2 pieces × 4$^3/_4$ inches (D)
    2 pieces × 2$^1/_2$ inches (E)
    2 pieces × 2$^3/_4$ inches (F)
Wood glue for outdoor use
Brads
Screws
Exterior primer
Exterior enamel paint
Hobby paint

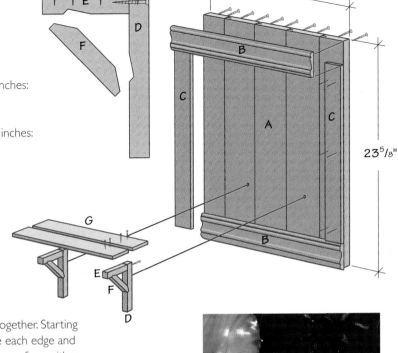

Here's what you do:

1. Lay the tongue-in-groove boards A together. Starting from the center, measure 8 inches to the each edge and mark the outer boards. Saw away the excess from either side to keep a symmetrical look to the boards.
2. Place A together again and lay mouldings B on top. Mark and cut the mouldings so they're flush with the edges of the panel. Glue and screw on the mouldings (from the back). Both mouldings should stick a little bit above and below the ends of the tongue-in-groove boards, leaving 1 foot 6 $^1/_2$ inches between them.
3. Cut, glue and nail the vertical trim C between the mouldings B.
4. Pre-drill brackets D and E to avoid splitting the wood when fastening. Glue and screw together brackets D and E. Let the glue dry.
5. Trim bracket support F to shape.
6. Place F over D and E and mark where D and E should be notched. Saw D and E.
7. F should fit tightly between D and E. Glue F in place and clamp it until the glue is dry.
8. Carefully glue and screw together the shelf boards G on the brackets. Do not attach to the sign at this point.
9. Paint the sign and shelf parts with primer. Once the parts are dry, paint them with enamel paint.
10. The text is painted with craft paint. Prepare a printout with the text you want. With a soft pencil outline the text on the reverse of the printout. Place the paper on the picture and re-draw the lines on the front. This will transfer the pencil marks on the reverse to the sign so you can paint in the letters.
11. Attach the shelf with two screws from the back.
12. Attach hooks and anything else you may want to the sign.
13. Drill holes in the sign for hanging.

Growing Cabinet

Here we have realized the "greenhouse dream" for the little garden, the balcony or for anybody who has enough space but perhaps too little time to care for flowers. My friend Cecilia has a small garden and a great interest in flowers, and we built this growing cabinet for her. The location was an obvious choice! It would stand against the raw, plastered wall facing the neighbor's back yard. The contrast was beautiful! The wall really enhances the cabinet, and as a bonus the family got a new, cozy coffee corner.

Materials

10 - 2 x 2 Boards (1^1/$_2$ x 1^1/$_2$ inches) x 8 feet, cut as follows:

    2 pieces x 68 inches (A)

    2 pieces x 60^9/$_{16}$ inches (B)

    2 pieces x 13 inches (C)

    1 piece x 39 inches (D)

    1 piece x 39 inches (E)

    1 piece x 36 inches (F)

    1 piece x 36 inches (G)

    2 pieces x 18^5/$_{16}$ inches (H)

    4 pieces x 57^7/$_8$ inches (J)

    4 pieces x 16^1/$_4$ inches (K)

    2 pieces x 16^3/$_4$ inches (L)

    1 piece x 16^3/$_4$ inches (M)

    1 piece x 36 inches (N)

    1 piece x 39 inches (O)

Stop Moulding, ^{1}/$_4$ x 1 inch:

    1 piece x 57^7/$_8$ inches (U)

Tongue-in-groove board, ^{3}/$_4$ x 3^1/$_2$ inches, approx. 59 feet:

    19 pieces x 36^1/$_2$ inches (P)

Dimensional planed lumber, ^{5}/$_8$ x ^{5}/$_8$ inch, approx. 13 feet 1 inch:

    10 pieces x 15^3/$_4$ inches (Q)

Dimensional planed lumber, ^{3}/$_4$ x 4^3/$_4$ inches, approx. 36 feet 1 inch:

    10 -12 pieces x 35^3/$_4$ inches (R)

Roof shutter support, ^{1}/$_4$ x 1 inch, approx. 2 feet 7 inches:

    2 pieces x 13^3/$_4$ inches (T)

Plexiglas, ^{1}/$_8$ inch:

    2 pieces x 16^3/$_4$ x 17^3/$_4$ inches (S1)

    6 pieces x 18^7/$_8$ x 16^3/$_4$ inches (S2)

    2 pieces x 20^3/$_4$ x 13^5/$_8$ inches (S3)

    4 pieces x 18^7/$_8$ x 13^5/$_8$ inches (S4)

    1 piece x 8^2/$_3$ x 13^5/$_8$ inches (S5), split into two sheets of Plexiglas

Hinges: 6 pieces with screws

Sliders with screws

Screws, 6 x 3 inches

Brads

Brads or glazer points

Wood glue for outdoor use

Exterior paint

Window putty

Here's what you do:

You will need a table saw or circular saw for this project. It is very important that all miter cuts be made at exactly the correct angle, and it is advisable to use a miter saw.

1. Start by cutting the grooves in parts A, F, B, C, H, J, K, L, M and O, sawing the 22.5 degree chamfer in O and G. This is most easily done by using a table saw.

2. Cut the miters on the ends of the studs as the construction progresses.

3. When assembling the frame and doors, use glue and screws. Drill pilot holes and recess the screws. Always check that the construction is square by measuring the diagonals.

4. Cut a 22.5° bevel on the top of A. Assemble side panel parts A, B and C. Repeat with the second side panel.

5. Cut a 22.5° bevel on the end of H. H should butt up against A with the top edge of H ^{3}/$_8$ inch down from the top of A. Position H and mark where the other end should be cut to connect to B. Cut H to length and assemble.

6. Connect the side panels with:

    D, which should connect to the A posts with the groove facing downward at the back edge;

    E, which should connect to the front of the B posts;

    F, which should attach between the side panel assemblies with the groove facing upward at the back edge;

    G, which should be connected between the two H parts.

7. Put the entire structure with the front down and attach the tongue-in-groove boards P. Do not glue the tongue-in-groove boards together, instead put a little glue in the grooves of A, D and F. Nail or screw with small screws pointed at an angle into the studs since the groove is only ^{3}/$_8$ inch wide.

8. Glue and screw on the shelf supports (strips Q) using small screws. Install them at heights that work for your pots.

9. Assemble the door parts J and K. Fix the strip U on back edge of one door, this functions as a stop for the other door.

10. Attach hinges to the doors and then to parts B.

11. Assemble O and L for the roof shutter. Then glue and screw N between the L parts.

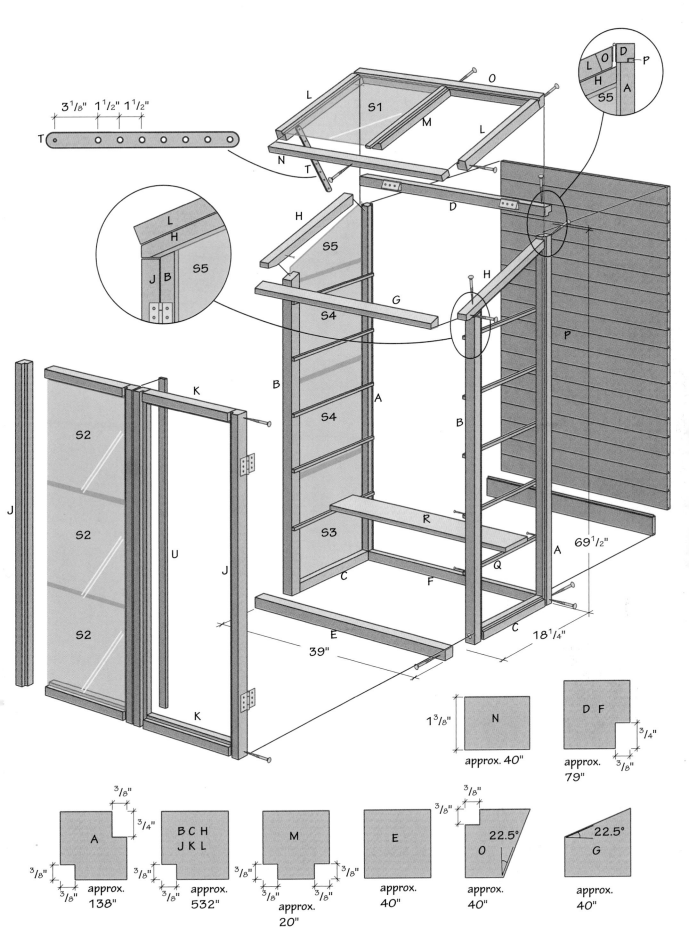

$3^1/8"$ $1^1/2"$ $1^1/2"$

T

L

O

S1

M

L

O

D

P

L

O

H

A

S5

N

T

H

L

H

S5

J B

D

S5

H

G

S4

B

S5

B

A

S4

H

P

J

S2

K

S2

S2

U

J

R

S3

A

Q

C

F

E

C

18 1/4"

69 1/2"

39"

K

1 3/8" N approx. 40"

D F 3/4" approx. 79" 3/8"

A 3/8" 3/4" 3/8" approx. 138"

B C H J K L 3/8" 3/8" approx. 532"

M 3/8" 3/8" 3/8" approx. 20"

E 3/8" approx. 40"

O 3/8" 22.5° approx. 40"

G 22.5° approx. 40"

12. On one end of M saw a 1 and $^3/_4$ inch tongue so that the part between the grooves remains and M will fit on top of N.

13. Glue and screw M at the middle of O and N.

14. Attach the hinges to the roof shutter and D.

15. Drill a $^3/_{16}$ inch hole at one end of each roof shutter support (T) and seven $^3/_8$ inch holes along the remainder of each support. Round the support ends.

16. Screw shutter support to L using the small hole in T. Locate the supports so they will fit inside O when folded up against the glass. Drive a nail into L so that the shutter supports can be held against L when not in use. Drive screws into H. They should be slightly smaller than the shutter support holes. The holes in the supports fit over these screws to hold the shutter open.

17. Drive four nails partway into the bottom of the shelves R to keep the shelves from sliding side to side. The nails should be positioned two at each end and located inside the strips Q when the shelves are in place.

18. Paint all surfaces with exterior paint and let the paint dry.

19. It is now time to fit the Plexiglas sheets. Cut the Plexiglas to size and check the fit of the piece in each opening. Squeeze a string of putty into the grooves and carefully press the sheet into place. Nail a few small brads or glazer points to hold the sheets in place. The Plexiglas S5 is cut at a 22.5° angle.

20. When all Plexiglas sheets are fitted, squeeze a string of putty into the groove and smooth over. Let the putty dry.

21. Finish painting the cabinet with one more coat of paint, covering the putty with paint.

22. Install the shelves.

23. Place the cabinet on a concrete slab or other solid surface. Place the cabinet against a sunny wall. It is a good idea to fasten the cabinet to the wall, especially if it is a windy location.

Long Bench

A very useful bench for large garden parties.

And perhaps the world's longest liar's bench? With space for eight

adult "liars" and one dog, there is space for plenty of great stories.

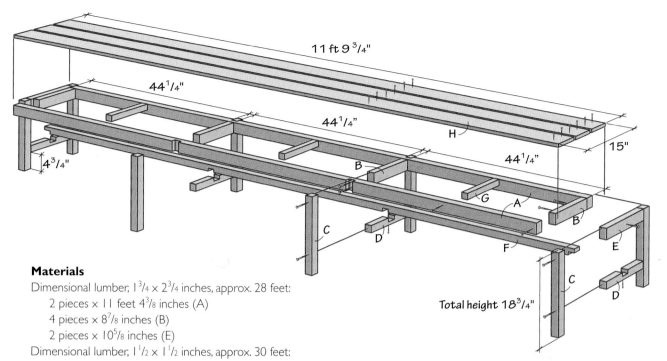

11 ft 9 ³/₄"

44 ¹/₄"

44 ¹/₄"

H

15"

44 ¹/₄"

B

G

A

4³/₄"

B

C

D

F

E

C

D

Total height 18³/₄"

Materials

Dimensional lumber, 1³/₄ x 2³/₄ inches, approx. 28 feet:
- 2 pieces x 11 feet 4³/₈ inches (A)
- 4 pieces x 8⁷/₈ inches (B)
- 2 pieces x 10⁵/₈ inches (E)

Dimensional lumber, 1¹/₂ x 1¹/₂ inches, approx. 30 feet:
- 8 pieces x 18 inches (C)
- 4 pieces x 10⁵/₈ inches (D)
- 1 piece x 11 feet 8 inches (F)
- 3 pieces x 8⁷/₈ inches (G)

Dimensional lumber for seats, ³/₄ x 4³/₄ inches, approx. 36 feet 1 inch:
- 3 pieces x 11 foot 9³/₄ inches (H)

Screws, #8 x 3¹/₂ inches and #6 x 2 inches
Wood glue for outdoor use
Wood filler for outdoor use
Shellac and wood sealer for exterior use
Primer and enamel paint for exterior use

Here's what you do:

Note: All screw holes should be countersunk and the screws sunk below the surface of the wood.

1. Saw and cut out the dados in the aprons A, for the legs C. The dados should be half the depth of the apron.
2. Glue and screw together both A pieces with the two middle cross bars B. Attach the legs in the dados with two screws. Position the two screws so that there is no screw in the middle. Make sure that the screws are recessed.
3. Glue and screw on the two outer cross bars B between the aprons A.
4. Glue and screw the four middle legs into the dados in A. The screws should be screwed into B between the screws that join A and B together.
5. Saw and cut out the half-lap joints in all the stretchers D to accept the longitudinal crossbar F. The half-lap joints should be half the depth of stretchers.
6. Assemble the two middle stretchers D between the two middle leg pairs C.
7. Glue and screw together the outer leg pairs, consisting of the parts C, E and D.

8. Glue and screw the outer leg pairs against A and B.
9. Put the longitudinal crossbar F in its place and mark where the half-lap joints should be located. Saw and cut out the half-lap joints in the longitudinal crossbar, making the half-lap joints half the depth of the stock. Glue F to D and drive a small screw through the bottom.
10. Attach the seat supports G with glue and screws.
11. Attach the seating boards H with glue and screws. First attach the middle board, and then the outer two, which should protrude ¹/₄ inch outside C.
12. Fill the screw holes with wood filler.
13. Sand any knots and coat with shellac.
14. Coat the bench with wood sealer.
15. Paint with primer, let the paint dry and sand lightly.
16. Finish off with two coats of enamel paint.

Woodshed

For a long time, our firewood was lying either in a pile on the driveway where it had been dumped by the supplier, or on the lawn under an ugly tarpaulin held in place by an old pallet. This had to be sorted out; we had to build a woodshed! We also found a use for the pallet (see the construction description). One important detail is that the woodshed does not require a building permit since it is built as a movable piece of "furniture". So if you later want to use it to refurnish the garden, simply get your wheel barrow out... but empty the shed of firewood first!

This little firewood shed is entirely beyond the reach of building permit regulations and garden shed regulations etc, since it is actually just a pallet with a superimposed structure that is easily moved around. Two people can easily carry the shed, and if you are on your own, you can move it with a wheel barrow.

If you want the shed to be detached, as opposed to attached to a wall, the back panel can be built like the sides, but the cross must remain to ensure lateral stability.

Materials

One pallet, cut to $31^{1}/_{2}$ inches × $47^{1}/_{4}$ inches
Dimensional lumber, $^{3}/_{4}$ × $4^{3}/_{4}$ inches, approx. 87 feet:
    10 pieces × $74^{5}/_{8}$ inches (A)
    2 pieces × approx. 65 inches (D)
    2 pieces × approx. $67^{3}/_{4}$ inches (E)
    1 piece × approx. $31^{3}/_{4}$ inches (F)
Dimension planed lumber, $1^{3}/_{4}$ × $2^{3}/_{4}$ inches, approx. 12 feet 5 inches:
    2 pieces × approx. 40 inches (B)
    2 pieces × approx. 32 inches (C)
Tongue-in-groove boards, $^{3}/_{4}$ × $3^{3}/_{4}$ inches, approx. 63 feet:
    12 pieces × approx. 61 inches (G)
Triangular strips, 2 × 2 inches, approx. 8 feet (H)
Dimensional lumber, $^{3}/_{4}$ × $3^{3}/_{4}$ inches, approx. 25 feet:
    2 pieces × $41^{3}/_{4}$ inches and 1 piece × 61 inches (J)
    2 pieces × $41^{3}/_{4}$ inches and 1 piece × $53^{1}/_{2}$ inches (K)
Roofing felt: 17 square feet
Roofing felt adhesive
Paperboard nail
Screws with different lengths
Exterior paint

Here's what you do:

1. Lay 5 of the side boards A next to each other with the bottom edges aligned and draw a 10° angle along the top face of the boards. This will create the pitch for the roof. Saw the angles.

2. Assemble the sides of the woodshed. Place each support B on a flat surface. Screw the A side boards to B. Note that the assembled side boards have a total width of $32^{3}/_{8}$ inches and there should be equal gaps between the sideboards.

3. Screw on middle support C so the support is flush with A at the front edge but approx. $^{3}/_{4}$ inch in from the back edge.

4. Screw both side assemblies to the pallet with long ($3^{1}/_{2}$ inches) screws. Make sure that the side assemblies are square to each other and hold them in place temporarily with a couple of cut-off strips screwed between the front edges of C.

5. Saw the parts D to rough measure, then hold them against the pallet and the sides and mark where the ends should be cut to form miter joints. Cut the miters, then hold

the D parts in place and mark where they overlap so you can cut the half-lap joints. To make the half-lap joints, saw several times with the circular saw to half the depth of the board and chisel out the waste. Screw the parts D to the assembly.

6. Cut the front trim parts E and F and screw them in place.

7. Attach the tongue-in-groove board G to the top edge of B. Start with the lowest part. Rip this board lengthwise to remove the tongue but otherwise, leave the tongue-in-groove boards at rough length and cut them off once in place. When you get to the last board on the back, rip it lengthwise to remove the groove and to make it flush with the back of B.

8. Rip the triangle strips H lengthwise so the two short legs are 2 × 2 inches. Then rip these strips in half to create the final pieces that create a neater look for the little roof (see detail on the drawing). Screw the H strips to the side and back edges of the tongue-in-groove.

9. Cut the roofing felt so it extends up the triangle strips. Then apply roofing adhesive to the tongue-in-groove and roll down the roofing felt.

10. Attach the windshields J to the sides and back of the roof and subsequently the roof trim K. It is a good idea to paint these boards before they are fitted in order to avoid spilling paint on the roofing felt.

11. Paint the little shed with your preferred color.

The little woodshed is easy to move around even if you are on your own.

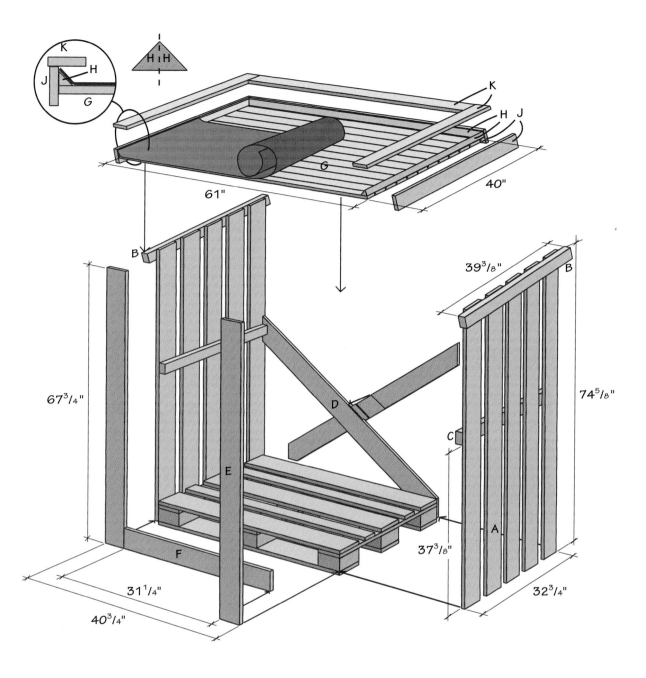

K
H
J
G

H | H

K

H J

61"

40"

39³/₈"

B

B

67³/₄"

74⁵/₈"

D

C

E

A

37³/₈"

F

31¹/₄"

32³/₄"

40³/₄"

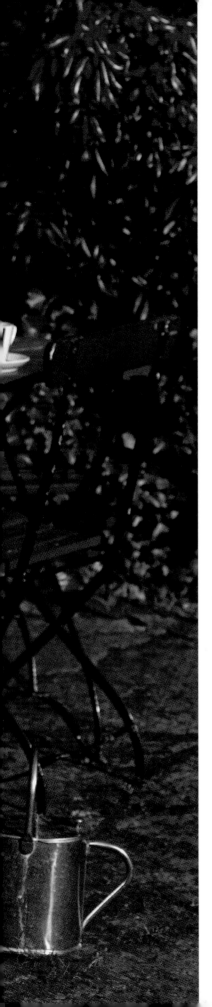

Planting Table with Sewing Machine Base

We love to recycle old things. This sewing machine frame belonged to the kids' paternal grandmother and was standing around idle in the garden shed for a long time. Now we use it as a planting table, and we feel it is a beautiful ornament in the garden. The upper part was built on two levels, in order for the table to be at a good working height, and also to make space for baskets, for garden trowels and pruning shears. The border, with the small shelf, adds 'snugness' to the table, improves proportions and prevents pots from falling off the sides.

Materials

Tongue-in-groove board, $^3/_4$ x $3^3/_8$ inches, approx. 66 feet:

    2 pieces x 30 inches (A1)
    4 pieces x 19 inches (A2)
    2 pieces x 18 inches (A3)
    2 pieces x 30 inches (B1)
    4 pieces x 19 inches (B2)
    6 pieces x $32^1/_4$ inches (C)
    6 pieces x $32^1/_4$ inches (D)
    2 pieces x $32^1/_4$ inches (E)

Wood glue for outdoor use
Wood screws
Machine screws
Shellac
Opaque glaze
Sewing machine base

7. Rip the edges of the outside boards lengthwise to remove the tongue and groove.

8. Screw the boards C into the side and back panels A.

9. Attach the side and back panels B by screwing from below at a slight angle.

10. Screw the bottom boards D into the side and back panels A.

11. Screw the top boards E on the side and back panels B.

12. Coat all knots with shellac to keep the oil in the knots from bleeding through.

13. Paint with semitransparent stain and bolt the table to the

Here's what you do:

1. Glue together two tongue-in-groove boards for the parts in the sides and backs, A and B. Cut the tongue and groove with a circular saw or table saw so that the sides and backs end up 6 inches high.

2. Cut the A and B parts to the correct lengths.

3. Lay out the curves on the side panels B2 and cut them out with a jigsaw.

4. Glue and screw together A1, A2 and A3.

5. Glue and screw together B1 and B2.

6. Cut the tongue-in-groove boards to length for the tops and bottoms C, D and E.

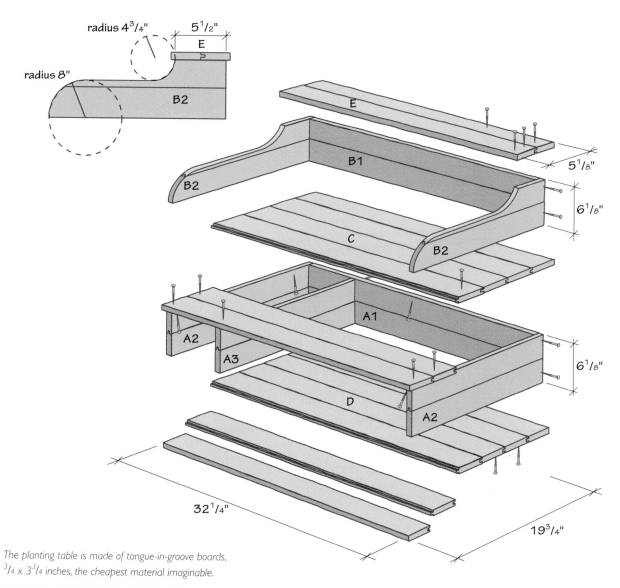

radius 4³/₄"

5¹/₂"

E

radius 8"

B2

E

B2

B1

5¹/₈"

6¹/₈"

B2

C

A2

A1

A3

A2

D

6¹/₈"

32¹/₄"

19³/₄"

The planting table is made of tongue-in-groove boards,
³/₄ x 3³/₄ inches, the cheapest material imaginable.

Table Tops on Metal Bases

Making new table tops is a cheap and simple way to use old heirlooms or flea market finds. Here we show another idea where we have used a sewing machine frame and an old table base made of wrought iron. The pillar table previously had a marble top which has unfortunately broken, but it was made useful again thanks to a round, wooden table top painted white. It is much easier than you might think to make a round table top.

Sewing Machine Base

Materials
Planed lumber, $^3/_4$ × $7^1/_4$ inches (1 × 8), approx.
8 feet 2 inches:
    3 pieces × $31^1/_2$ inches (A, B and C)
Screws, $1^1/_4$ inches
Wood glue for outdoor use
Glaze for outdoor use

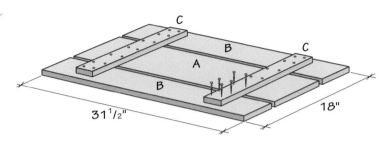

31$^1/_2$"   18"

Here's what you do:
1. Cut two of the boards lengthwise to a width of 5 inches. These are tabletop parts B. The cut-offs will be used as the supports C.
2. Cut the supports C to a length of 16 inches.
3. Put the tabletop boards A and B next to each other on a flat surface, with the good faces facing down. Place $^1/_4$-inch spacers, such as plywood scraps, between the boards to create even spacing.
4. Screw and glue on the supports C. Make sure the screws end up flush with the supports.
5. Sand and stain the table top.

Wrought Iron Base

Materials
Planed lumber, $^3/_4$ × $2^3/_4$ inches, approx. 20 feet:
    8 pieces × $23^3/_4$ inches (A)
    2 pieces × 23 inches (B)
Screws, $1^1/_4$ inches
Wood glue for outdoor use
Shellac
Priming and enamel paint for outdoor use

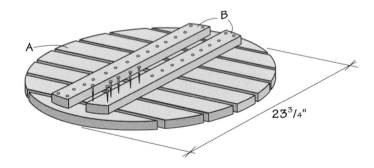

$23^3/_4$"

Here's what you do:
1. Lay all the boards A for the top on a flat surface with the good faces facing down. Put $^1/_4$-inch plywood spacers in between the boards.
2. Tape a small piece of cardboard over the gap in the middle of the top, then tack a nail in the center. Attach a string to the nail and then tie a pencil to the other end $11^7/_8$ inches from the nail. Use the pencil to draw a circle.
3. Lay the supports B in place. Make sure they are centered on the circle you drew.
4. Re-tie the pencil to the string $^3/_4$ inch closer to the nail. Then mark a radius on each end of the B supports.
5. Cut the ends of the supports (only the supports at this time) with a jigsaw.
6. Screw and glue the supports onto the boards A. Drill pilot holes for the screws at the ends of B to prevent the wood from splitting.
7. Turn the top over, find the center and draw a circle with a radius of $11^7/_8$ inches. Cut the top out with a jigsaw.
8. Coat all knots with shellac to prevent them from bleeding through.
9. Sand, prime and paint.

Side Tables

Our good friends wanted a side table for their patio. Since they often have guests over, sometimes in large numbers, the solution was to have one large and two smaller tables. The tables are a good height for serving food and for leaning against a little later in the evening. In order to fit in with the somewhat sparse environment, the design is simple. Once the party is over, the two smaller tables can be nested below the large one until the next time there are lots of guests.

Materials

Dimensional planed lumber, $1^3/_4 \times 1^3/_4$ inches, approx.
75 feet 5 inches:

- 4 pieces × 40 inches (A1)
- 4 pieces × $12^1/_4$ inch (B1)
- 3 pieces × $55^1/_2$ inches (C1)
- 8 pieces × $36^1/_4$ inch (A2)
- 8 pieces × $10^1/_4$ inches (B2)
- 6 pieces × $22^7/_8$ inches (C2)

MDF (medium density fiberboard) board, $^1/_2$ inch:

- 1 piece × $15^3/_4 \times 59$ inches (D1)
- 2 pieces × $13^3/_4 \times 26^3/_8$ inches (D2)

Galvanized sheet metal:

- 1 piece × $20^5/_8 \times 64$ inches (E1)
- 2 pieces × $18^5/_8 \times 31^1/_4$ inches (E2)

Glue for outdoor use
Screws, 4 $^1/_3$ inches
Screws, 1 $^1/_3$ inches
Wood filler for outdoor use
Shellac
Exterior primer
Exterior enamel

Here's what you do:

1. Saw leg, apron and stretcher parts A, B and C for all three tables. (You will achieve the straightest and best results by using a miter saw.)
2. Glue and screw together parts A and B to form the end assemblies for the three tables. Measure the diagonals so that the side panels are square.
3. Glue and screw the apron parts C to the end assemblies. Again, check diagonals to make sure the parts are square.
4. Glue and screw the MDF boards D to the table assemblies.
5. The sheet metal lids E should fit loosely on the tables. Since you will need special tools to cut and bend the steel, it may be easier to have a tinsmith or a metalworker make the table tops. If you go this route, leave the tables with the tinsmith to make sure the tops will fit.
6. Apply wood filler and sand the tables.
7. Coat all knots with shellac.
8. Paint with primer, sand lightly and finish painting with two coats of enamel.
9. Put the lids on.

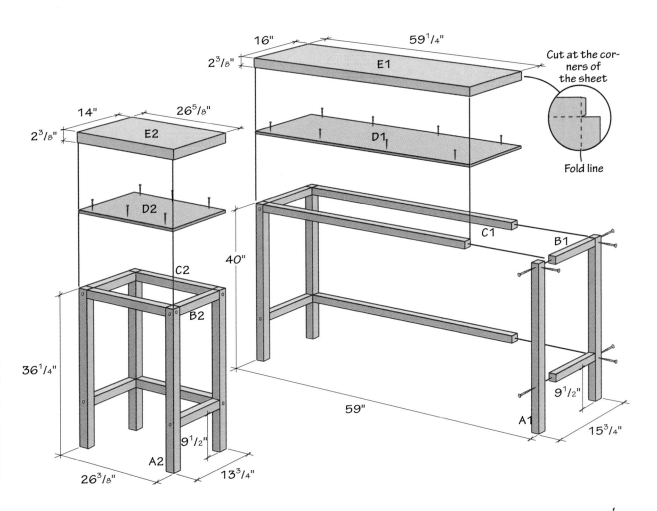

16"

59 1/4"

2 3/8"

E1

Cut at the corners of the sheet

14"

26 5/8"

2 3/8"

E2

D1

Fold line

D2

40"

C1

B1

C2

B2

36 1/4"

9 1/2"

A1

9 1/2"

A2

26 3/8"

13 3/4"

59"

15 3/4"

Garden Bench

This cute little bench is really comfortable to sit on since you can rest

your arms on the handles. It is perfect for moving around and sitting

on when the roses need cutting or you need a spare seat by the grill.

Materials

Stud, $1^3/_4 \times 1^3/_4$ inches, approx. 14 feet:
- 1 piece × $25^1/_4$ inches (A)
- 4 pieces × $8^1/_4$ inches (B)
- 4 pieces × $25^5/_8$ inches (C)

Dimensional planed lumber, $1^3/_4 \times 2^3/_4$ inches, approx. 6 feet:
- 2 pieces × $21^5/_8$ inches (D)
- 2 pieces × $12^5/_8$ inches (E)

Dimensional planed lumber, $3/_4 \times 2^3/_4$ inches, approx. 9 feet:
- 4 pieces × $25^1/_4$ inches (F)

Screws

Wood plugs

Wood glue for outdoor use

Wood sealer, primer, enamel paint.

Here's what you do:

1. Make the half-lap joints in the stretchers A and B1 by sawing halfway through each board then chiseling away the waste. Do not assemble the parts at this time.

2. Drill two dowel holes in each joint of B1, B2 and C. Glue dowels in the holes then reinforce each joint with one screw. This creates the two leg assemblies.

3. Fit together the leg assemblies in the same way with D. Be careful not to drill into the screw that connects B and C.

4. Glue the half lap joints in A and B1 then reinforce the joint with one screw from below through B1.

5. Cut out the seating boards F and make cutouts in the outer boards for the legs C according to the drawing. Glue and screw down the boards with even gaps between them.

6. Draw and cut out the handles E with a jigsaw. Sand thoroughly and round the edges.

7. Drill dowel holes in E and C assemble the joints with glue and dowels. Clamp these parts and let the glue dry.

8. Sand as much as you think is required. Then brush with wood sealer and leave to dry.

9. Paint one coat with primer and two coats with enamel paint.

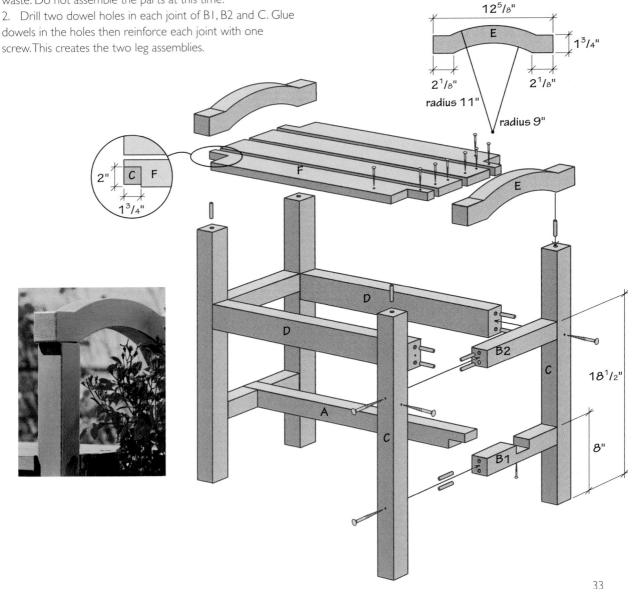

Awning

This awning was a real upgrade for the balcony and the bedroom inside. The proportions of the balcony were improved, and now the doors can be opened even if it rains without damaging the wood profiles on the doors or the parquet flooring inside. The tempered glass is very resistant and lets light through and, unlike plastic roofing, the pounding of the rain cannot be heard.

Our awning is fixed to a wall that has a frieze at the top. This complicated the construction of the awning. It is unusual for a frieze to be located so near the door, so here we have designed an awning for a smooth wall. There is, however, something to add about how we designed the awning to fit over a frieze. See the framed drawing.

Material
Dimensional planed lumber, $1^{3}/_{4} \times 4^{3}/_{4}$ inches, approx. 15 feet:

  2 pieces × 76 inches (A and B)
  2 pieces × approx. 8 inches (F)
Dimensional planed lumber, $1^{3}/_{4} \times 2^{3}/_{4}$ inches, approx. 29 feet 6 inches:

  2 pieces × $31^{3}/_{4}$ inches (C)
  2 pieces × approx. $31^{1}/_{8}$ inches (D)
  7 pieces × $32^{1}/_{4}$ inches (E)
Glass spacer strip, $^{1}/_{4} \times 1$ inch, approx. 5 feet 6 inches:

  2 pieces × $32^{1}/_{4}$ inches (H)
Glass spacer strip, $^{1}/_{4} \times {}^{3}/_{4}$ inch:

  1 piece × $32^{1}/_{4}$ inches (J)
Glass hold down, $^{1}/_{4} \times 1^{3}/_{4}$ inches, approx. 9 feet:

  3 pieces × $32^{1}/_{4}$ inches (K)
Dimensional planed lumber, $^{3}/_{4} \times 4^{3}/_{4}$ inches, approx. 5 feet 6 inches:

  2 pieces × 33 inches (L)
Tempered glass, $^{1}/_{8}$ inch:

  2 pieces × $32^{7}/_{8} \times 36^{13}/_{16}$ inches (G)
Screws
Wood glue for outdoor use
Lag screws
Rubber strip
Shellac
Primer for outdoor use
Enamel paint for outdoor use.

Here's what you do:
The construction of the entire structure except G, H, J, K and L is completed before installing the awning to the wall.
1. Saw and chisel half-lap joints in ledger A and joist B.

that the roof should be tilted 7°, so the half-laps must be cut at 7°. Also cut a 7° miter at both ends of E. The half-laps should be sufficiently deep but should leave the E roof beams projecting above A and B by $^{1}/_{8}$ inch or so.
3. Screw the E roof beams that are directly above the C pillar into A. Make sure they are fixed at a 7° angle.
4. Saw a cutout in the top of the C pillar so it fits around A, This will create a tongue on C. When C is installed the tongue should be flush with E and slightly angled to follow the angle of E. Attach C to A.
5. Clamp support D to C and E to form a 45° angle as shown in the detail drawing. a. Mark the shape on D where D will intersect E and C.
6. Unclamp D and cut the shape.
7. Clamp D again and mark on C and E where D intersects these two pieces.
8. Remove D and saw the notches on C and E.
9. Screw joist B to the two roof beams E that are installed.
10. Put both D parts where they should be and fasten them with a screw or two.
11. Screw on the other E parts.
12. Hold the supports F behind E and C and mark with a pencil where to cut the miters. Cut the supports F, glue and screw them on.
13. Coat knots with shellac. Prime and paint the entire structure. Also take the opportunity to paint H, J, K and L.
14. Attach the wood structure with lag bolts through C and A. You'll need to drill holes in the assemblies and wall for the lag bolts. The holes in the assemblies should be slightly larger than the bolts so they can turn freely, and the holes in the wall should be slightly smaller than the bolts so the bolts will hold firmly. The wall determines the size of the lags you'll need to use.
15. Attach the H spacers with a few small nails on the outer E, and nail the J spacer on the middle E. Put a thin rubber strip next to these on E. Lay the glass sheets G and put a rubber strip on these above the other rubber strip. Screw on the K hold down.
16. Cut and screw on the L trim pieces on both sides.
17. Finish painting where needed.

Modifications for roof against profiled wall

Additional Material, or material that has different measurements:
Dimension planed lumber, $1^{3}/_{4} \times 1^{3}/_{4}$ inches:

  1 piece × 76 inches (A1)
Dimension planed lumber, $1^{3}/_{4} \times 2^{3}/_{4}$ inches, approx. 23 feet:

  2 pieces × $31^{1}/_{8}$ inches (C)
  7 pieces × $29^{1}/_{2}$ inches (E)
Front panel board, $^{3}/_{4} \times 4^{3}/_{4}$ inches, approx. 5 feet 2 inches:

  2 pieces × $30^{5}/_{16}$ inches (L)
Tempered glass, $^{1}/_{8}$ inch:

  2 pieces × $30^{1}/_{8} \times 36^{3}/_{4}$ inches (G)
2. Saw and chisel half-lap joints in the roof beams E. Note

Here's what you do:
1. Measure up the profile on your wall and adjust measurements accordingly.
2. When you have sawed the half-laps in A (point 1), screw A1 on A.
3. C is screwed on with one screw from above through A1.

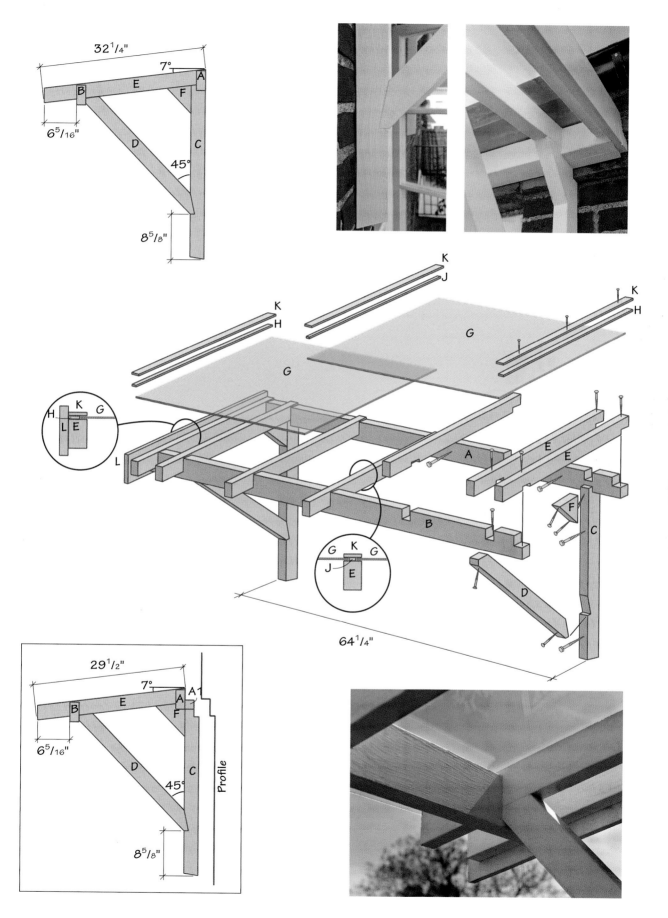

32¹/₄"

7°

A

B

E

F

6⁵/₁₆"

D

C

45°

8⁵/₈"

K

J

K

H

K

H

G

G

H

K

G

L

E

L

A

E

E

G

K

G

J

E

F

C

B

D

64¹/₄"

29¹/₂"

7°

A

A

B

E

F

6⁵/₁₆"

D

C

45°

8⁵/₈"

Profile

Tray with Handles

A tray for summer coffee or small pots with seedlings. It is lovely, so I think we will have to make several of them since it is often used as a beautiful still life. This tray also makes a nice gift for friends — loaded with cheese, crackers, fig jam and a bottle of wine.

Materials

Lathing strips, $^3/_8 \times 1^3/_4$ inches, approx. 16 feet:
   2 pieces × $19^3/_4$ inches (A)
   2 pieces × $10^1/_4$ inches (B)
   5 pieces × $19^3/_4$ inches (C)
   2 pieces × $12^5/_8$ inch (D), ripped into 4 pieces with a
   width of approx. $^7/_8$ inch.
Dowel rod, @ $^1/_2$ inch diameter:
   1 piece × $19^3/_4$ inches (E)
Wood glue for outdoor use
Brads
Screws
Exterior primer
Exterior enamel paint
Paste wax

Here's what you do:

1.   Glue and nail together the frame,
consisting of A and B. Drill pilot holes in A to
avoid the wood splitting and to guide the
nails.
2.   Glue and nail the boards C on the bottom of the
frame. Drill pilot holes in C.
3.   Place the arms D in the correct position facing each
other and mark for cutting the half-lap joints. Saw and chisel
out the half-laps. Glue the parts together and clamp until the
glue is dry.
4.   Round the tops of D. Drill pilot holes for the screw to
connect to the handle E. Glue and screw the arms to E.
5.   Glue and screw D to B, first drilling pilot holes in D.
6.   Paint the whole tray with primer.
7.   Apply enamel paint with a cloth. Leave the tray to dry.
8.   Sand with fine sandpaper until the parts look suitably
worn. Sand mostly the edges and corners and the handle.
9.   Rub the entire tray with paraffin oil.

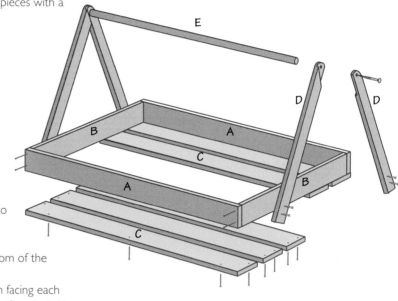

Doorway Trellis

Our friends, who live in a town-house with neighbors close by, wanted a screen to provide some privacy near the entrance door. It was important to them that it should feel airy and that plants could grow on it. The solution was a simple trellis painted white with green leaves striving upwards all by themselves.

This trellis is fitted to the steps by the entrance. It is fixed to the ceiling and to the wall by the stairs. Adapt your trellis according to the measurements of your house.

Materials

Dimensional planed lumber, $3/4 \times 1 3/4$ inches, approx. 46 feet:

    6 pieces × 79 inches (A)
    2 pieces × $34^1/4$ inches (B)

Lathing strips, $3/4 \times 3/4$ inch, approx. 9 feet:

    3 pieces × $34^1/4$ inches (C)

Screws
Wood glue for outdoor use
Exterior paint

Here's what you do:

1. The three C braces should be evenly spaced over the vertical strips A. To locate them, put all A parts together and hold them with some clamps. Mark where the C braces should be fixed. Saw all A parts at the same time to create dados for the braces, this is most easily done with a circular saw set at the correct depth. Chisel out the waste after you saw.
2. Screw and glue on the bottom brace B1 and the top brace B2. Make sure that all A parts are evenly distributed along B. Drill pilot holes in B to attach the A parts, then screw the parts together, two screws in each vertical strip.
3. Drill pilot holes, screw and glue the C braces.
4. Paint with exterior paint.

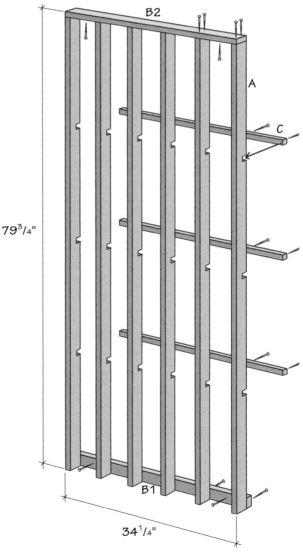

B2

A

C

$79^3/4$"

B1

$34^1/4$"

Planting Table for Kids

Imagine having your own planting table when you were a kid! One that looks like Mom and Dad's, only a little smaller. Getting to plant and help out "for real" when seedlings have grown roots in a glass of water in the window and need to be planted, is a dream come true.

Materials

Dimensional planed lumber, $^3/_4 \times 1^1/_4$ inches, approx. 21 feet 3 inches:

- 4 pieces × 20$^3/_8$ inches (A)
- 4 pieces × 14$^7/_8$ inches (B)
- 4 pieces × approx. 13$^1/_2$ inches (C)
- 2 pieces × approx. 24$^{13}/_{16}$ inch (D)

Dimensional planed lumber, $^3/_4 \times 1^3/_4$ inches, approx. 8 feet 2 inches:

- 4 pieces × 24 inches (E)

Tongue-in-groove board for shelves, $^3/_4 \times 3^3/_8$ inches, approx. 9 feet 2 inches:

- 5 pieces × 20$^7/_8$ inches (F)

Dimensional planed lumber, $^3/_4 \times 2^3/_4$ inches, approx. 12 feet 5 inches:

- 2 pieces × 17$^1/_8$ inches (G)
- 4 piece × 22$^1/_2$ inches (J)
- 2 pieces × 4$^1/_8$ inches (K)
- 1 piece × 9$^7/_8$ inches (L)

Dimensional planed lumber, $^3/_4 \times 7^3/_4$ inches:

- 1 piece × 22$^1/_2$ inches (H)

Screws

Brads

Wood putty

Wood glue for outdoor use

Shellac

Wood sealer

Exterior primer and enamel paint

Here's what you do:

1. Glue and screw together two frames made of parts A and B, first drilling pilot holes in A.
2. Glue and screw the apron C onto B. Make sure the apron is of equal distance from each end of B.
3. Glue and screw the legs E onto the frames.
4. Lay the table frame on a flat surface with the front of the assembly facing down. Make sure all angles are at 90°. Place the D diagonal supports on top, adjust them into the correct position and mark where they overlap so you can cut the half-lap joints.

5. Saw and chisel the half-lap joints in both D parts. Put them together and place the cross on the table frame again. Mark where D should be mitered at the ends. Cut the miters.
6. Glue the diagonal parts together, then glue and screw the braces to A with a screw in each of the four corners.
7. Cut the tongue-in-groove boards F for the table top. The front and back boards should be sawed lengthwise to remove the tongue and groove. The back part should reach just up to the inner edge of A without resting on A. The front part should protrude $^3/_8$ inch beyond A. Glue and nail F to the table assembly.
8. Round one of the corners of the rim boards G using a $2^3/_4$ inch radius. Glue and screw each into the end grain of the table top.
9. Saw the panel for the backboard H so that it fits exactly between the rim boards G. Attach the backboard with glue and screws, screwing through H and into F and through G and into H.
10. Saw notches in the front shelf board J to fit around the legs and glue and screw it to the frame. Attach the back shelf board J. It should rest against E. Attach the rest of the boards with even gaps between them.
11. Saw shelf brackets K so that they are $2^1/_2$ inches wide at the top. Glue and screw shelf L to the brackets.
12. Glue and screw this small shelf to the backboard H. The screws are screwed in from the back.
13. Apply wood putty as needed and sand.
14. Coat knots with shellac.
15. Apply one coat of wood sealer and let it dry.
16. Apply one coat primer and two coats enamel paint.

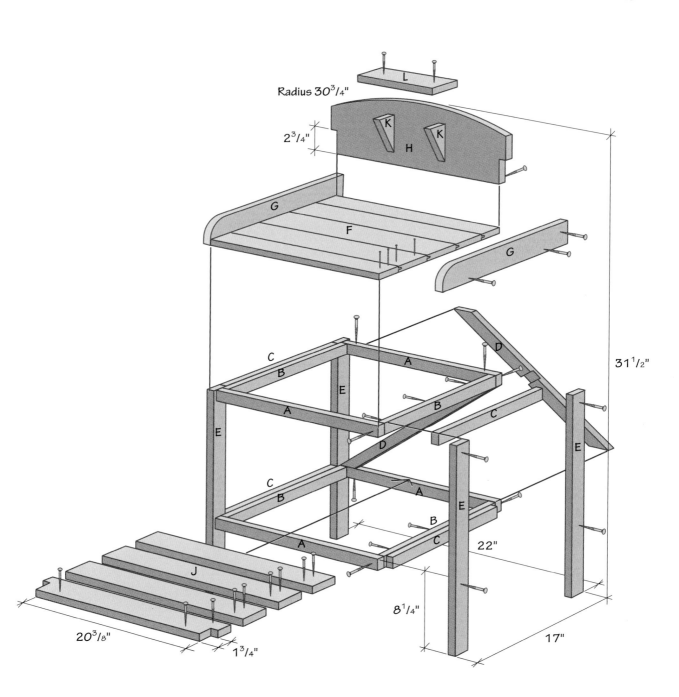

Radius 30³/₄"

L

K K
H

2³/₄"

G

F

G

31¹/₂"

C
B
A
E
A
D
B
C
D
E
C
B
A
E
B
A
C
J
E
B
C
22"

20³/₈"

1³/₄"

8¹/₄"

17"

Minibench

Yes, we are very keen on benches of all kinds. There should be plenty of seats in a garden.

This is the smallest one we have ever built, and with its thick, squat profiles it is absolutely

the cutest one (if you can call a garden bench cute?). We also like to be able to vary things

by putting "garden furniture" like this indoors, for example in the bathroom.

Materials

Dimensional planed lumber, $1^3/_4 \times 11^3/_4$ inches:
    1 piece $\times$ $23^5/_8$ inches (C)
Dimensional planed lumber, $1^3/_4 \times 8^3/_4$ inches,
approx. 2 feet $3^1/_2$ inches:
    2 pieces $\times$ $11^3/_4$ inches (D)
Dimensional planed lumber, $1^3/_4 \times 3^3/_4$ inches,
approx. 2 feet $3^1/_2$ inches:
    2 pieces $\times$ $11^3/_4$ inches (E)
Dimensional planed lumber, $1^3/_4 \times 2^3/_4$ inches,
approx. 3 feet 3 inches:
    1 piece $\times$ $15^3/_4$ inches (A)
    2 pieces $\times$ $11^1/_8$ inches (B)
Wood dowels: 3 pieces
Wood glue for outdoor use
Screws, $3^1/_2$ inches: 10
Wood filler for outdoor use
Shellac
Exterior primer and enamel paint

Here's what you do:

Note that all screw holes should be counter-sunk
and the screws set below the surface of the wood.
1. Saw the B supports with each end double-
mitered at a 45° angle.
2. Assemble the B and A parts with glue and
wood dowels. Clamp and let the glue dry.
3. Put C upside down, with the finished support
assembly (A and B) centered on C. Position the D
parts and glue and screw the D parts into A.
4. Turn the assembly over and glue and screw on
the seat C.
5. Mark how the feet E should be sawed and use
a compass to draw the radiuses. Cut with a jigsaw
and sand.
6. Turn the mini-bench upside down, glue and
screw on the feet.
7. Sand and apply wood putty over all screw
heads.
8. Coat all knots with shellac. When the shellac
has dried, prime and lightly sand the bench.
9. Finish off with two coats of paint.

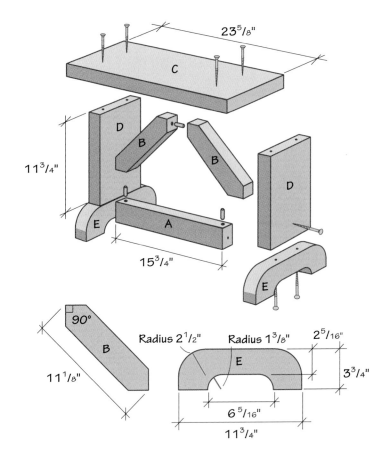

Why not put the bench inside?

Deck with Privacy Fence

Imagine stepping out barefoot on a wood deck warmed by the sun. When we designed and built this deck, the owner wanted it to be large to surround the house and be protected from prying eyes by privacy fencing, and yet feel open and welcoming. Obviously, it had to fit in with the existing environment and the newly built house.

The result was a very generous wood deck measuring 592 square feet with enough space for dining furniture, a grill, a sofa group and a reading corner – and yet large areas remain vacant.

The patio described here is very large, see the drawing below. Adjust your patio according to your own preferences.

This description only includes a few measurements, and no numbers, since the material should be adjusted to the patio on site.

The patio's left side is not visible on the drawing on the next page, but is assembled in the same manner. The part of the patio which is visible on the right on the drawing is considerably shortened. Rough-cut lumber is used for supports P and the slats O are planed on three sides and sawed on one.

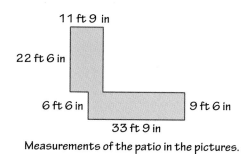

Measurements of the patio in the pictures.

Materials

Non-woven landscape fabric

Sand or gravel

Concrete piers with saddle brackets, bolts and nuts

Paving stones

Water-resistant sheeting

Pressure-treated lumber, $2^3/_4 \times 2^3/_4$ inches:

    Post 69 inches (A)

    Spacer block $4^3/_4$ inches (G)

Pressure-treated lumber, $1^3/_4 \times 4^3/_4$ inches:

    All studs in the frame (B, C, D, E, F, H, J, K and L)

Rough-sawed lumber, $^7/_8 \times 1^3/_4$ inches,

    for mounting strips (P) × 63 inches

Rough-sawed lumber, $^7/_8 \times 2^3/_4$ inches,

    for slats, 18 pieces per section (O)

Timber decking, pressure-treated, 1 × $4^3/_4$ inches (M)

Nailing plates

Joist hangers

Angle brackets

Lag screws

Wood screws

Decking screws

Exterior paint

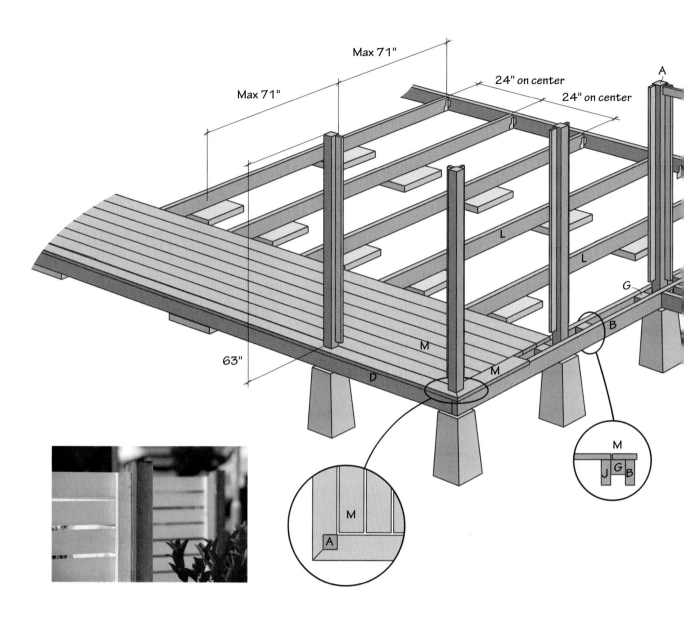

Here's what you do:

1. Dig holes for the concrete piers. Each hole should be 8 inches deeper than the height of the pier. Fill it with gravel to the level where the base of the pier should rest. Pack well. Install the pier and level it carefully, measure and put up a brick line. Pack stones and gravel around the pier to hold it in place. Make sure you turn the pier so that the U-shaped saddle metal bracket is correctly positioned. See the drawing.

2. Remove soil to a depth of about 4 inches in the areas that will be under the deck. Cover the ground with non-woven landscape fabric, cover with approx. 2 inches of gravel and pack down the gravel.

3. Lay down paving stones as support points for the deck joists. Make sure the paving stones are at the correct height in relation to the piers.

If joists B and C cannot be bolted to the side of the house, there should be a row of paving stones alongside the house as well to support these joists.

Carefully check that the paving stones are level with a spirit level or laser level.

4. Bolt the A posts to the piers.

5. Screw joist B to the house with lag screws (or put it on paving stones). B continues out from the house and rests on a paving stone, and is then screwed to the A posts. The B joist is long and will need to be spliced. Attach a nailing plate at the splice to hold the ends of the spliced joists together. Make sure the plate does not interfere with any of the joist hangers that you'll need to install later. Also screw the D joists to the posts.

At the corners, the U-shaped saddle brackets on the piers

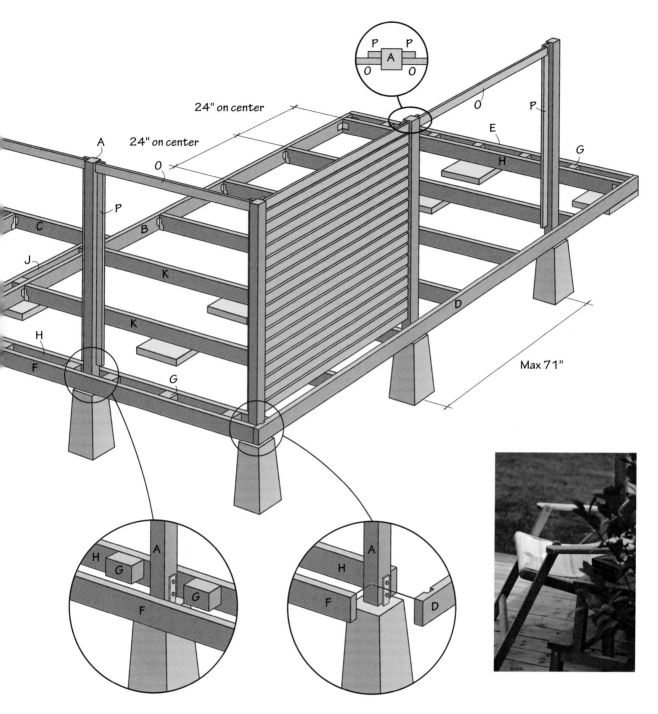

will interfere with the joists. Cut off one leg of each bracket. Also, cut dados in B and D so that they will fit over the saddle bracket and B and D can be screwed directly into A.

B and D will partly rest on paving stones as well. Place water-resistant sheeting between the paving stones and lumber everywhere.

6.   Bolt the C joist to the house and screw it to B.

7.   Screw the F joist into two of the A posts and to B.

8.   Attach the E joist to B and D, using framing brackets to reinforce. The brackets must be smaller than $2^3/_4$ inches.

9.   Screw the G spacer blocks into the B, E and F joists.

10.   Screw the floor joists H and J into the A posts, and into the spacer blocks and the B, C, D and F joists.

11.   Attach joist hangers to B, C and D and nail the floor joists K and L to these.

12.   Lay down the timber decking M. Start by framing the perimeter of deck, except alongside the house, see the drawing. Miter the corners and saw cutouts for the poles. Always cut the decking so it ends over a joist for support.

13.   Saw and screw on the rest of the decking. Begin with the part visible on the right in the drawing. Begin from the outside and continue inwards toward the house. The last board will probably need to be sawed lengthwise. Never place two spliced decking boards next to each other and do not let any board cover more than three joists.

Screw the decking onto the other part of the patio.

Template for assembly of slats.

O

14. Paint all the P nailing strips and O slats before they are attached.

15. Screw the nailing strips onto the A posts.

16. Screw on the upper slat O in all sections. Use a spirit level and be meticulous.

17. Make two templates for spacing the remaining slats O. Cut two strips approx. 5 feet 6 inches long. Screw 18 screws into each strip. The upper screw should rest above the upper slat O, the other screws should be below the remaining slats. See the drawing on the right and the photo on p. 76.

18. Hang the templates with the upper screw resting on the upper O, then put the slats in place step by step and screw them on. Move the templates to the next section etc.

Birdhouses

Building birdhouses is easy and fun for both kids and adults.

You need to know the size of the house, the diameter of the entrance hole and what direction

the birdhouse should face. This all depends on what birds you would like to attract.

The materials description includes three alternative birdhouses and specifies the birds for which they are suitable.

Materials

Birdhouse 1 – *flycatcher, tufted titmouse*
Dimensional planed lumber,
  $3/4 \times 4^3/4$ inches, approx. 52 inches
  $3/4 \times 1^3/4$ inches, 24 inches

Birdhouse 2 – *house sparrow, tree sparrow*
Dimensional planed lumber,
  $3/4 \times 5^3/4$ inches, approx. 36 inches
  $3/4 \times 4^3/4$ inches, approx. 30 inches
  $3/4 \times 1^3/4$ inches, 24 inches

Birdhouse 3 – *black-capped chickadee, Carolina chickadee*
Dimensional planed lumber,
  $3/4 \times 5^3/4$ inches, approx. 52 inches
  $3/4 \times 4^3/4$ inches, approx. 6 inches
  $3/4 \times 1^3/4$ inches, 24 inches

Screws
Nails
Perhaps a rope

Here's what you do:

1.   Cut all the parts. A, E and C are cut at a 22.5° angle against the broadside of the board at one end. One side of B is cut at a 22.5° angle. The unplaned side should always be turned inwards so that the birds can get a grip.
2.   Drill the access hole Y in C. This is most easily done with a hole saw.
3.   Screw both sides B to back piece A. Screw front piece C to B and the mounting board F to A.
4.   Cut the bottom D. It should fit loosely with a gap all around, partly so the bottom will be easy to open, and partly to drain the birdhouse of water. Drill pilot holes at the lower end of B to make it easier to drive the screws. Hold D at the correct position and put the screws in through B. Do not

screw too tightly; it should be possible to open the bottom. Hold D in position and drill one hole through C into D. Insert a nail, which can be easily removed when the birdhouse needs to be cleaned.
5.   Screw the roof E on.
6.   Drill pilot holes into the mounting board F for the installation. The holes can be drilled from the front for installation with screws if you're mounting it on the facade of the house. Trees can be damaged if you drill or screw into them. To avoid this, drill holes through the side of F so you can thread a rope through and loosely tie the birdhouse around the tree just above a branch. (Both holes are visible on the drawing.)

		Birdhouse 1	Birdhouse 2	Birdhouse 3
A	Dimensional planed lumber:			
	$^3/_4 \times 5^3/_4$ inches		$12^{13}/_{16}$ in	$14^1/_8$ in
	$^3/_4 \times 4^3/_4$ inches	$10^1/_{16}$ in		
B	2 pieces ×			
	$^3/_4 \times 5^3/_4$ inches			$13^3/_4$ in
	2 pieces ×			
	$^3/_4 \times 4^3/_4$ inches	$9^3/_4$ in	$12^1/_2$ in	
C	$^3/_4 \times 5^3/_4$ inches		$10^5/_8$ in	$11^3/_8$ in
	$^3/_4 \times 4^3/_4$ inches	$7^7/_8$ in		
D	$^3/_4 \times 4^3/_4$ inches	$3 \times 4^1/_2$ in	$4 \times 4^1/_2$ in	$4 \times 5^1/_2$ in
E	$^3/_4 \times 5^3/_4$ inches		$9^7/_8$ in	$10^7/_8$ in
	$^3/_4 \times 4^3/_4$ inches	$8^5/_8$ in		
F	$^3/_4 \times 1^3/_4$ inches	$17^3/_4$ in	$20^1/_{16}$ in	$21^5/_8$ in
X	Distance to the hole:	$5^3/_4$ in	$6^3/_4$ in	$8^3/_4$ in
Y	Diameter of hole:			
	flycatcher	$1^1/_4$ in		
	tufted titmouse	$1^1/_4$ in		
	house sparrow		$1^3/_8$ in	
	tree sparrow		$1^1/_4$ in	
	black-capped chickadee			$1^3/_8 - 1^9/_{16}$ in
	Carolina chickadee			$1^1/_8 - 1^1/_8$ in

Position the birdhouse at the correct height above ground, facing the intended direction:

flycatcher	6 ft 6–9 ft 9 in; S, E
tufted titmouse	6 ft 6–9 ft 9 in; S
house sparrow	6 ft 6–9 ft 9 in; S, E, W
tree sparrow	6 ft 6–9 ft 9 in; S
black-capped chickadee	8 ft 2 $^4/_{10}$–9 ft 9 in; S, E, W
Carolina chickadee	6 ft 6 in; S, E

In order for the birds to come back year after year, it is important to clean the house after each season. Just pull out the nail and open the bottom to clean the birdhouse.

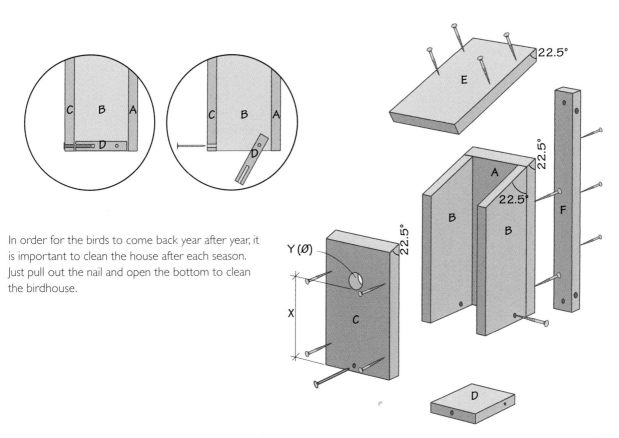

Bird Feeder

I keep this bird feeder just outside my office window, and I often look at it when I'm working. It is fun and amazingly soothing to watch small birds.

Materials

Plywood, $^{1}/_{4}$ inch:

    1 piece × 11 × 11 inches (A)

    2 pieces × 6 × 7$^{3}/_{4}$ inches (D1)

    2 pieces × 6 × 8$^{1}/_{4}$ inches (D2)

    2 pieces × 10$^{3}/_{8}$ × 14$^{9}/_{16}$ inches (F1)

    2 pieces × 11 × 15$^{3}/_{8}$ inches (F2)

Dimensional planed lumber, $^{1}/_{2}$ × $^{1}/_{2}$ inch, approx. 30 inches:

    4 pieces × 6 inches (E)

Dimensional planed lumber, $^{1}/_{4}$ × 1 inch, approx. 54 inches:

    4 pieces × 15$^{3}/_{8}$ inches (B)

Dowel, @ $^{3}/_{8}$ inch diameter, approx. 5 feet:

    4 pieces × 12$^{5}/_{8}$ inch (C)

Triangle strip, $^{1}/_{2}$ × 1$^{1}/_{4}$ inches, approx. 40 inches:

    4 pieces × 8$^{3}/_{8}$ inches (G)

Post (H) – we used a fallen branch, but you can also use a post, $^{3}/_{4}$ × $^{3}/_{4}$ inch, as shown in the drawing.

Wood glue for outdoor use

Screws

Finishing nails

Exterior paint

Lag screw: 1 piece

Roofing felt

Asphalt cement

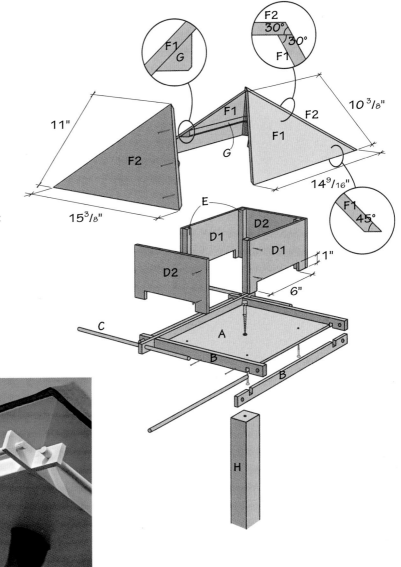

Here's what you do:

1. Saw the bottom A and drill a hole in it for the lag screw.
2. Saw and chisel out the half-lap joints in all strips B. Measure so that the inner measurement of the frame B is consistent with A.
3. Drill pilot holes for the dowel rods a short distance in from the ends of B.
4. Assemble B with a little glue. Insert the bottom A, glue and nail it in place.
5. Insert the dowel rods C; attach them with a little glue.
6. Saw the opening in the bottom edges of D1 and D2. Screw and glue D1 onto the corner strips E. Repeat with D2. This forms the feeder box.
7. Cut out the triangular parts F1 and F2, which will form the roof. Note that the F2 pieces are slightly longer than the F1 pieces. At the bottom all the F1 and F2 pieces should be beveled at a 45° angle and at the sides at a 30° angle.

8. Bevel the inside top edges of the F2 pieces so they will fit tightly at the top.
9. Glue and nail one F2 piece against the other F1 pieces. Glue and nail on the next F2.
10. Lay the roof F upside down and insert the D feeder box. Mark on the inside of F where the G strips should go to hold the roof evenly above the feeder box. Saw the G strips to length; glue and screw them onto F.
11. Glue and fix the feeder box onto the bottom A using screws from below into E.
12. Cut and attach the roofing felt with asphalt glue. Fix the felt with a staple gun where needed.
13. Paint the bird feeder with your preferred color.
14. Screw the bird feeder onto the post H and put the roof on, which fits loosely.

Sun Bed

On a trip to the Caribbean, we stayed in a hotel with wide sun beds everywhere – in the open, large reception area, by the pool and on the beach. They were covered with cushions and many had a square shape, thatched roofs and were raised a little. So inviting!

I felt a strong urge for something similar here at home. So, inspired by this trip, we built our version. Our sun bed is 48 inches x 79 inches, has a foldable backrest – and plenty of cushions! It has become a very popular piece of furniture in our house – occupied by lounging teenagers as soon as the weather permits.

Materials

Stud, $1^3/_4 \times 1^3/_4$ inches, approx. 35 feet:

    2 pieces × $51^1/_4$ inches (A)

    4 pieces × $43^3/_4$ (B)

    2 pieces × $23^5/_8$ inches (C)

    4 pieces × $17^3/_4$ inches (D)

Stud, $1^3/_4 \times 4^3/_4$ inches, approx. 2 feet 3 inches:

    2 pieces × $12^5/_8$ inch (E)

Lathing, $^3/_4 \times 1^3/_4$ inches, approx. 17 feet:

    3 pieces × $51^3/_{16}$ inches (F)

    2 pieces × $20^1/_{16}$ inches (G)

Dimensional planed lumber, $^3/_4 \times ^3/_4$ inches, approx. 23 feet:

    2 pieces × $51^3/_{16}$ inches (H)

    1 piece × $51^3/_{16}$ inches (J)

    46 pieces × 3 inches (K)

Dimensional planed lumber, $^3/_4 \times 2^3/_4$ inches, approx. 70 feet 6 inches:

    19 pieces × $43^{11}/_{16}$ inches (L)

Dowel rod, @ $^1/_2$ inch diameter, approx. 1 foot 7 inches:

    2 pieces × 6 inches (M)

Wood dowels: 52 pieces

Screws of various dimensions

Wood glue for outdoor use

Hinges: 2 pieces

Shellac

Exterior primer

Filler for outdoor use

Exterior enamel paint

Here's what you do:

Note that all screw holes should be counter-sunk and the screws set below the surface of the wood.

1. Drill dowel holes for the dowels at one end of each of the K parts.

2. Mark on A and B1 where K should be fixed, then drill dowel holes for the dowels there too.

3. Glue together all parts K and A. Glue together all parts K and B1. Clamp and let the glue dry.

4. Cut H and J so they are the same length as A and B1 respectively. Glue and screw H and J onto all K parts, first drilling pilot holes. Make sure the K parts are at a 90° angle to the parts above and below them. Let the glue dry.

5. Mark and drill dowel holes in the ends of H and D. Screw and glue together D and A. Drill pilot holes and recess the screws. At the same time, glue the dowels between H and D.

6. Fasten the side panel parts B1 and J in D in the same way.

7. Screw and glue B2 between the legs D to complete the frame.

8. Screw and glue together the B3 and C parts.

9. Screw and glue the F1 support strips into A and the G support strips into C.

10. Attach the hinges to the bed and the backrest with screws.

11. Mark and saw both parts E with a jigsaw. Drill pilot holes in the face of E to attach it to the backrest and drill evenly spaced adjusting holes in the side. These holes should be sized so your dowel rod will fit snugly.

12. Glue and screw E onto the bottom of G. Also screw it to B3. Make sure the E parts move freely in between the D legs.

13. Coat all knots with shellac. Let the shellac dry and prime the entire structure and the L slats and F2.

14. Glue and screw the L slats, evenly distributed, into F1 and G, respectively.

15. Turn the entire bed upside-down, glue and screw F2 into L. F2 should not be attached to B1 and B2.

16. Apply wood putty over all screw heads and any uneven surface. Sand.

17. Apply two coats of enamel paint.

18. Place the dowel rod M in the holes in E to set the backrest angle.

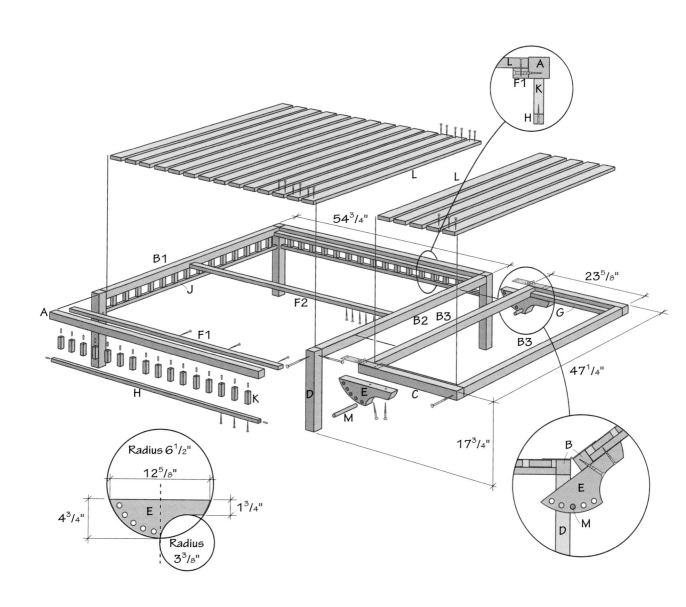

L A
F1 K
H

L L

54³/₄"

B1

J

F2

23⁵/₈"

A

F1

B2 B3

G

B3

H K

D E C

M

17³/₄"

47¹/₄"

B

E

D M

Radius 6¹/₂"

12⁵/₈"

4³/₄"

E

1³/₄"

Radius 3³/₈"

Patrick's Bench

We call it Patrick's bench since it was built for my brother Patrick.
The bench looks complicated to make but is easy to build if you have a miter saw.
As an extra detail, the legs and crossbars are joined with reinforcing bars. Today the
bench finally stands where it belongs – on Patrick's jetty by a lake.

Materials

Pressure-treated lumber, $1^3/4 \times 4^3/4$ inches, approx. 18 feet:
- 4 pieces × $19^3/4$ inches (A)
- 3 pieces × 42 inches (D)

Pressure-treated lumber, $1^3/4 \times 1^3/4$ inches, approx. 5 feet 6 inches:
- 2 pieces × $11^3/4$ inches (B)
- 1 piece × $39^3/8$ inches (C)

Reinforcing bars, @ $3/8$ inch diameter, approx. 2 feet:
- 2 pieces × $8^5/8$ inches (E)

Screws: 3 inch 16 pieces
Wood glue for outdoor use
Wood sealer

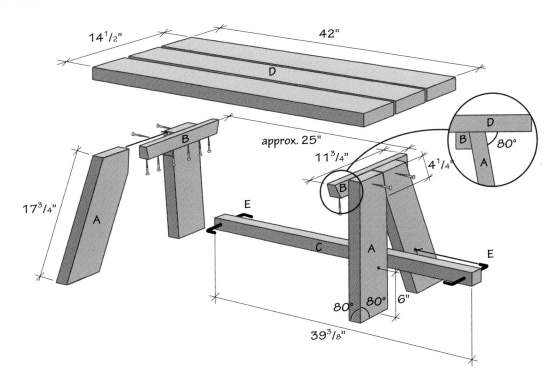

Here's what you do:

1. Set your miter saw at a 10° angle and 10° tilt and cut the tops and bottom edges of all four legs A.

2. Pair two legs together so that they are in the position in which they should be assembled. Along the top edges, draw a line at a right angle to locate the miter you will cut so the edges of the legs will touch when the legs are splayed (see the measurements in the drawing). Set the saw at a right angle and without a tilt, and cut a wedge off each leg.

3. Glue together the pairs of legs A, clamp them and let the glue dry. (Use the wedges that you cut off to get a grip with the clamp.)

4. Cut two supports B. Miter the ends at a 10° angle. Also saw them at a 10° angle lengthwise.

5. Screw and glue the supports B onto the pairs of legs A.

6. Drill a $3/8$ inch hole approx. 1 inch from each end of the stretcher C.

7. It can be difficult to bend the reinforcing bars E, but if you put them in a vise it is easy. First bend one end of each bar ($1^1/8$ inches), insert into the hole in C and bend the other end ($1^1/8$ inches).

8. Lay your seat boards D on a flat surface and temporarily clamp the pairs of legs upside down. Move the pairs of legs back and forth until they fit and mark where the holes in A for the reinforcing bars should be. Drill with a $5/16$ inch drill approx. $1^3/8$ inches deep into each leg.

9. Assemble the pairs of legs A and the stretcher C between them by driving in the reinforcing bars E.

10. Put the boards for the seat in a row, evenly spaced, with the good side facing up. Place the leg structure upside down on top of these, measure exactly where the legs should be fixed. Drill pilot holes, glue and screw the leg structure onto D.

11. Apply several coats of wood sealer.

Fencing with Trellises

A fence could hardly be more stable than this one, since it is built with corners to ensure stability even through the most violent autumn storms. The corners, with their open sides, ensure that the fence doesn't feel too closed in, while the cozy "bays" offer natural space for small flowerbeds. Next year the "bays" will be filled with winding plants and flowering bushes.

Materials

Gravel

Concrete piers with saddle brackets, bolts and nuts

Pressure-treated lumber, $2^3/_4 \times 2^3/_4$ inches:

   Posts × 64 inches (A)

   Posts × 45 inches (B)

Pressure-treated lumber, $1 \times 1^3/_4$ inches, with rounded corners as timber decking:

   2 pieces per high section × 62 inches (C1)

   2 pieces per high middle section × 62 inches (C2)

   1 piece per high section × 62 inches (C3)

   2 pieces per low section × 43 inches (D1)

   2 pieces per low middle section × 43 inches (D2)

   1 piece per low middle section × 43 inches (D3)

   15 pieces per low section × 63 inches (E)

   42 pieces per high section × 63 inches (E)

   6 pieces per low middle section × 11 inches (F)

   8 pieces per high middle section × 11 inches (F)

Galvanized wood screws

Materials for pier template

Boards, $3/_4 \times 3^3/_4$ inches, approx. 17 feet:

   2 pieces × 79 inches (a)

   2 pieces × $23^5/_8$ inches (b)

Rebar: 1 piece for each pier, × approx. $11^3/_4$ inches

Materials for template to install slats

Strip, $1/_2 \times 1/_2$ inch, approx. 19 feet 8 inches:

   2 pieces × approx. 66 inches for the high section

   2 pieces × approx. 47 inches for the low section

Screws

8" gravel or shingle, tightly packed

Here's what you do:
Setting the Piers

1. Build a template for placing the cement piers, see drawing below.

2. Glue and screw together pier template parts a and b.

3. Carefully measure where the holes for the reinforcing bars should be. Drill pilot holes for the reinforcing bars into the b pieces, as shown.

4. Draw a line in the middle between the holes, see the red line.

5. Put up a brick line (string level) along the border of the garden or through the middle of the area where the fencing will go. Put the template in place so that the brick line is exactly in front of the template's middle line. Insert a length of rebar in each hole. Lift the template and move it one template length, cover the two rebars with it and insert the next pair. Continue along the entire fencing. Now all the piers have been located.

6. Dig or, preferably, drill holes for the piers. You can rent an auger.

7. Each hole should be approx. 8 inches deeper than the height of the pier. Fill it with gravel to the base of the pier. Pack well. Put down the piece and adjust it carefully, place the template over it again, the board b should be between the bars, which should touch a. Keep the template in place while you tamp gravel around the pier.

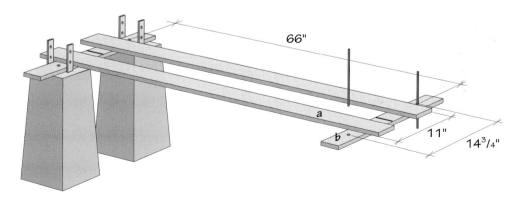

66"

a

b

11"

14³/₄"

Template for placement of plinths.

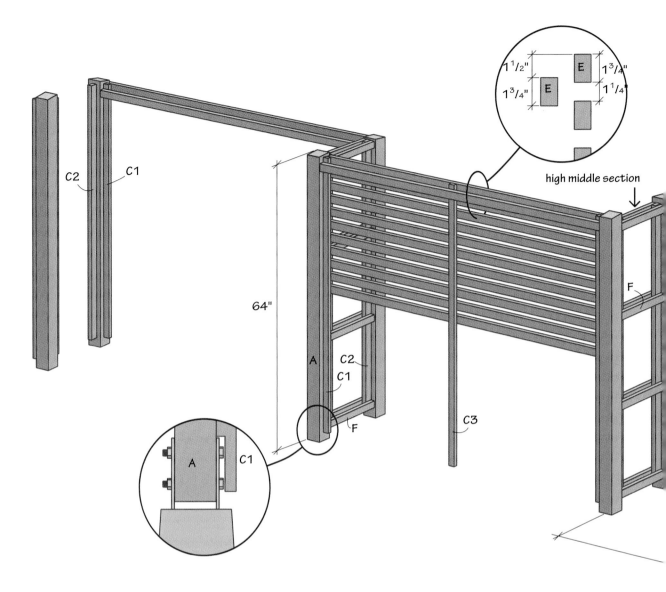

C2 C1

64"

A C2
C1

F

C3

$1\frac{1}{2}$"

$1\frac{3}{4}$"

E

E

$1\frac{3}{4}$"

$1\frac{1}{4}$"

high middle section

A C1

F

Template for placement
of slats.

E

Building the Fence

8. Saw the top of posts A and B at an angle so rainwater will drain off.

9. Attach the A posts to the saddle brackets on the piers. It is important that the posts are at the correct height. First fit the outer pairs of posts, run a string level between them and then place the remaining posts following the line. Continue in the same way with the B posts.

10. Screw the spacer strips C1 and C2 onto the posts A and the spacer strips D1 and D2 onto the posts B.

11. Screw on the two upper E parts, one on each side, with offset of $1\frac{1}{2}$ inches between the parts (see the drawing). Check continuously with a spirit level that the posts are straight.

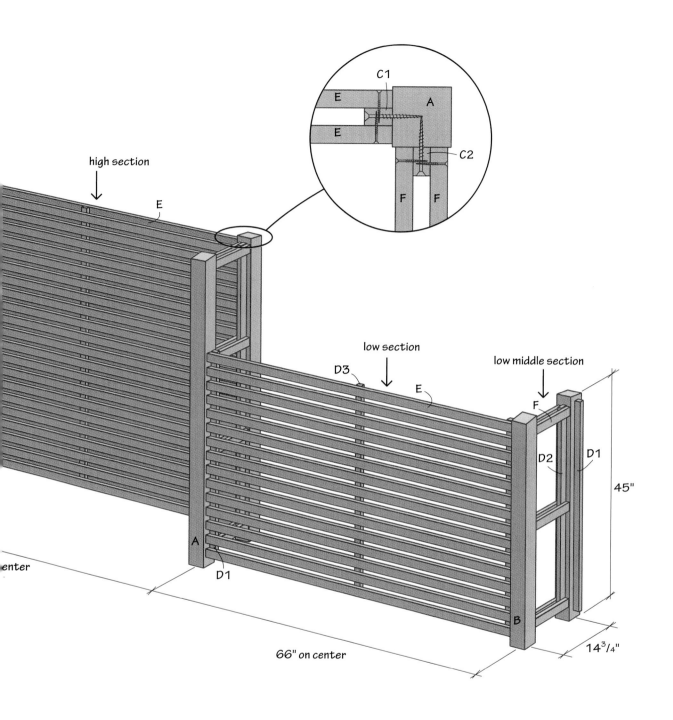

high section

C1

E

A

E

C2

F F

low section

low middle section

E

D3

F

E

D2

D1

45"

center

A

D1

B

66" on center

14³/₄"

12. Build two templates for the assembly of the remaining slats E, see separate drawing.

Saw two thin strips to size. Screw 21 screws into each strip for the high section and 15 screws for the low section. The upper screw should rest on the upper slat E, and the other screws should be spaced evenly so each falls below the remaining slats E.

Hang the template with the upper screw resting on the upper E, then put the slats in place step by step and screw them on.

13. Attach the spacer strips C3 and D3 to the middle of the fitted E slats using screws.

14. When you have completed one side of the fence, turn the templates and continue with the other side. The slats will quickly and easily fit at the correct height. For a more open feeling, the low sections has slats only on one side.

15. Attach the trellis strips F on C2 and D2 using screws. The upper I strips should be level with the upper E slats and the lower strips should be level with the lower E slats. Distribute the remaining F strips evenly in between.

Hanging Box

I wanted a hanging herb garden for our outdoor dinner table so I could reach over and cut fresh herbs for the food. When we finished building the herb box, we realized that it could also be used as a beer cooler. Our guests thought it was a fun detail on the dining table at midsummer's lunch.

Materials

Dimensional planed lumber, $5/8 \times 5^3/4$ inches, approx.
5 feet:
  2 pieces $\times 19^3/4$ inches (A)
  2 pieces $\times 5^3/4$ inches (B)
Strips, $3/4 \times 1^1/4$ inches, approx. 13 feet:
  2 pieces $\times 5^3/4$ inches (C)
  3 pieces $\times 18^1/2$ inches (D)
  2 pieces $\times 8^3/8$ inches (E)
  2 pieces $\times 21$ inches (F)
  2 pieces $\times 9^1/2$ inches (H)
Rebar, @ $3/8$ inch diameter, approx. 3 feet 3 inches:
  2 pieces $\times 17^3/4$ inches (G)
Screws
Wood glue for outdoor use
Plastic liner (plastic sheeting or a garbage bag)
Exterior paint

Here's what you do:

1. Glue and screw together parts A and B.
2. Glue and screw the strip C $3/4$ inch from the bottom edge onto side panel B.
3. Glue and screw the bottom boards D to the strip C. Distribute them evenly.
4. Saw the frame strips E and F to create half-lap joints at the ends. Glue together, clamp and let the glue dry.
5. Put the plastic liner in the box, fold the ends so that the box is sealed. Fasten the liner with a staple-gun on the upper side of A and B. Cut off the leftover so nothing pokes out.
6. Place the frame E and F on top and screw it down. (The frame is easy to remove if you need to change the plastic.)
7. Saw a $3/8$ inch deep and $3/8$ inch wide track into the strips H. Drill pilot holes and screw H to the underside of the table. Check with the box to make sure the H strips are at the correct distance from each other.
8. Paint the box with exterior paint.
9. Slot the reinforcing bars G into the tracks on H and put the box in place.
10. Remember to make a few holes in the plastic for drainage.

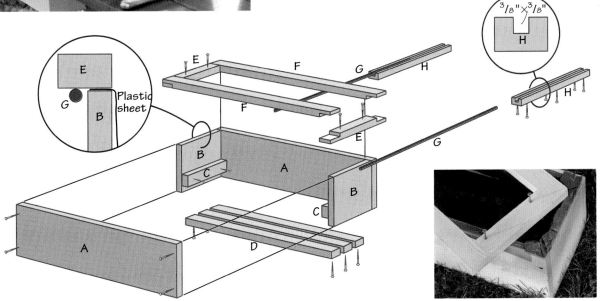

Washbasin

Cooking, washing the dishes or washing outside can be soothing and calming, as a contrast to the stresses of modern life — work, school, electronics and fast food. Often, we live a simpler existence in the summertime. Small, practical chores are allowed to take as long as they need. No obligations or priorities get in the way, except perhaps what book to read in the hammock after breakfast.

Also, I finally found a use for at least part of my collection of enameled containers. Not everyone is a proud owner of a bunch like this, but you can take whatever you might have stashed away, go to a flea market and search for bargains or buy something new if you prefer.

Materials

Dimensional planed lumber, $^3/_4 \times 1^3/_4$ inches, approx. 41 feet:

    2 pieces × 36 inches (A)

    2 pieces × 53 inches (B)

    4 pieces × approx. 28 inches (D)

    4 pieces × 16 inches (E)

    4 pieces × $21^3/_4$ inches (F)

    2 pieces × $18^1/_4$ inches (G)

Dimensional planed lumber, $^3/_4 \times 2^3/_4$ inches, approx. 16 feet 4 inches:

    4 pieces × $14^1/_4$ inches (C)

    2 pieces × $5^1/_2$ inches (L)

    2 pieces × $5^1/_2$ inches (N)

    5 pieces × $21^3/_4$ inches (J)

Rough-sawed lumber, $^3/_4 \times 3^3/_8$ inches, approx. 20 feet 4 inches:

    6 pieces × $21^3/_4$ inches (H)

    5 pieces × $21^3/_4$ inches (K)

Dimensional planed lumber, $^3/_4 \times 4^3/_4$ inches:

    1 piece × 25 inches (M)

Dowel rod, @ $^1/_2$-inch diameter:

    1 piece × $17^3/_4$ inches (O)

Wood dowels, $^1/_8 \times 1^1/_2$ inches: 32 pieces

Screws

Brads

Wood putty

Wood glue for outdoor use

Shellac

Wood sealer

Exterior primer enamel paint

Here's what you do:

1. Cut the side apron boards C to length and put two of them 24 inches apart on a workbench or table. Make sure they are parallel and facing each other. Fasten them with clamps.

2. Place the D parts over the C parts so they criss-cross and the outside edges of the D parts align with the edges of the C parts. Mark where the D parts should be sawed to create half-lap joints and cut the joints.

3. Put the parts D together forming a cross. Place them over C again and mark where the ends should be mitered to fit flush against C. Saw the miters.

4. Glue together the crosses D, make sure they fit flush against C. Clamp them and let the glue dry.

5. Drill dowel holes in D and C and assemble them with wood dowels and glue. Clamp the parts and let the glue dry.

6. Set your side assembly against A and B and mark where to drill dowel holes. Drill the holes and assemble the parts with dowels and glue. Clamp the parts and let the glue dry.

7. Cut out the two N brackets with a jigsaw. Put them together and drill the hole for the round dowel rod O. Glue and screw the brackets to the face of one pair of legs A and B. They should be centered laterally on the legs.

8. Glue and screw the strip E on the inside of C. E and C should be flush at the bottom. E is longer than C and should protrude equally on both sides.

9. The two side panels are now ready. Fit them together with the four F parts. Glue and screw onto E.

10. Glue and screw the mounting boards G against the legs B.

11. Glue and nail the front panel boards H onto G. The lower and the upper boards should be sawed lengthwise so they're equal in width.

12. Glue and nail the shelf boards J onto E. The front and back boards should protrude a little over F. Make sure they are evenly spaced.

13. Glue together the edges of the boards K to form one top. Draw a circle which fits the washbasin you will use. Cut out the hole using a jigsaw. Make the cut before you attach the basin panel to the stand. Otherwise, the C boards and the panel H are in the way.

14. Attach the basin panel using glue and nails. Remember that the top should protrude approx. $^3/_8$ inch beyond the front frame board F.

15. Cut out and attach the brackets L using screws and glue at the top of the legs B.

16. Attach the shelf M using glue and screws. The shelf should protrude approx. ¹/₄ inch beyond the front edge of the brackets. Also make sure that it extends by the same amount beyond each bracket.

17. Insert the dowel rod O into the brackets N and fix it with a dollop of glue. It should extend equally beyond both brackets.

18. Apply wood putty as needed and sand.

19. Coat all knots with shellac.

20. Apply one coat of wood sealer and let it dry.

21. Apply one coat of primer and two coats of enamel paint.

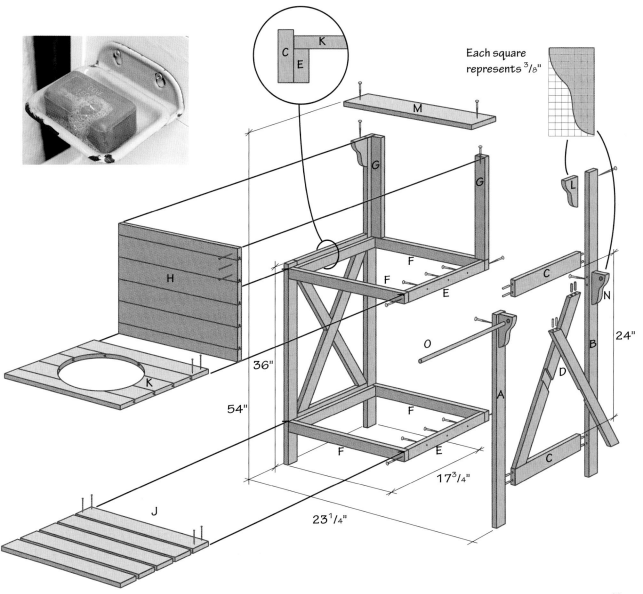

Wall Trellis

A trellis made of the cheapest material imaginable, un-planed furring strips and rebar,

and with movable shelves for trinkets and flowers. The idea is that it should look like

a "painting" with plenty of odd, rusty items and winding plants.

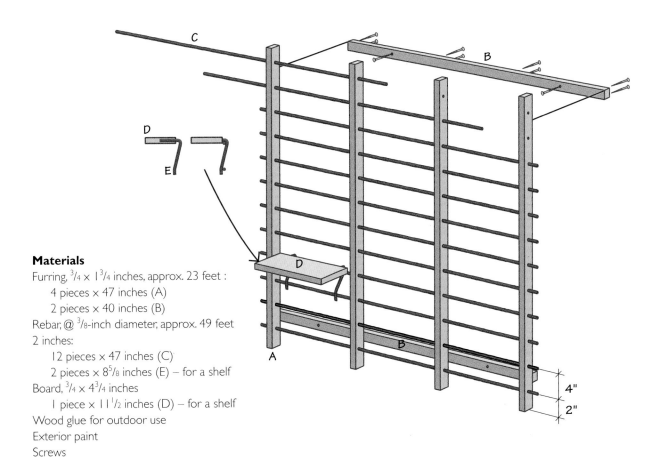

Materials

Furring, $^3/_4 \times 1^3/_4$ inches, approx. 23 feet :
 4 pieces × 47 inches (A)
 2 pieces × 40 inches (B)
Rebar, @ $^3/_8$-inch diameter, approx. 49 feet
2 inches:
 12 pieces × 47 inches (C)
 2 pieces × 8$^5/_8$ inches (E) – for a shelf
Board, $^3/_4 \times 4^3/_4$ inches
 1 piece × 11$^1/_2$ inches (D) – for a shelf
Wood glue for outdoor use
Exterior paint
Screws

Here's what you do:

1. Drill pilot holes for the rebar C in all the boards A. The holes should be large enough that the rebar fits easily.
2. Drill pilot holes, then glue and screw the strips B to the backs of A.
3. Paint the structure before the rebar is installed.
4. Install all the rebar.
5. Drill pilot holes in B for hanging and fit the trellis on the wall.

6. Drill two deep holes on the reverse of the shelf D. The rebar E should fit tightly into these holes.
7. Paint the shelf D before installing the rebar.
8. Bend E, preferably in a vise. Experiment to get the right angle so that the shelf will be level.
9. Press or hammer the reinforcing bars E into the shelf D.

Box for Storage

All the cushions used in our garden and patio were kept in a pile behind the sofa in the living room whenever the dew was likely or the rain came. Completely unacceptable!

You can get great, water-resistant plastic boxes that come cheap, but we feel that they don't fit visually in our home. There are also beautiful wooden boxes that will withstand a shower of rain. They look good, but are expensive – and we would have needed two of them.

So, we built a wooden box long enough to conceal two very practical plastic boxes and with some space left over for pots. As a bonus, we got a nice, new bench below the window where we can sit and mull over new carpentry projects!

Materials

T1-11, $^3/_4$ × 4$^3/_4$ inches, approx. 138 feet:

    12 pieces × 116 inches (A)

    12 pieces × 20$^1/_2$ inches (B)

Dimensional planed lumber, $^3/_4$ × 3$^3/_4$ inches, approx. 31 feet 2 inches:

    10 pieces × 25 inches (C)

    2 pieces × 53$^1/_4$ inches (F)

Stud, 1$^3/_4$ × 1$^3/_4$ inches, approx. 7 feet 2 inches:

    2 pieces × 20$^1/_2$ inches (D)

    2 pieces × 19$^3/_4$ inches (E)

Dimensional planed lumber, $^3/_4$ × 2$^3/_4$ inches, approx. 17 feet 4 inches:

    6 pieces × 24 inches (G)

    16 pieces × 59 inches (J)

Dimensional planed lumber, $^3/_4$ × 1$^3/_4$ inches, approx. 14 feet 9 inches:

    8 pieces × 21$^3/_4$ inches (H)

Wood glue for outdoor use

Hinges: 4 pieces

Wood sealer

Exterior paint

Plastic boxes for storing cushions

Here's what you do:

1. Saw off the tongue at the top of the upper T1-11 boards A and B.

2. Place two boards C and the boards B on top of these to form a side panel. At each corner, one of the C boards should protrude by the thickness of A (see inset drawing). At the bottom each C board should protrude by approx. $^3/_4$ of an inch. This will keep the paneling from coming into contact with the ground. Glue and screw together the parts. Screw from the inside of the box. Continue in the same way with the other side panel.

3. Repeat for the boards A and C on the long side. C should protrude by as much as the thickness of C. Do not attach the middle C.

4. Glue and screw the side panels to the long sides with long screws (3 inch).

5. Measure the middle of the long side and attach the studs D using glue and screws, with long screws through A. Screw and glue on the studs E.

6. Attach the middle boards C with glue and screws from the inside of the box along the sides of E.

7. Screw and glue the boards F along the upper edge of the back of cabinet. The F boards fit between the C boards.

8. Put the G parts in place. The two parts in the middle should be $^1/_4$ inch apart.

9. Glue and screw on the lid boards J. There should be a $^1/_4$ inch gap between them in the middle. On the front and the side, the panels J protrude over G by a fraction of an inch.

10. Flip the lids over and glue and screw on the strips H.

11. Flip the lids back and fit each lid with two pairs of hinges on the strip H and the board F.

12. Apply wood sealer to the lower part of each C part and let the sealer dry. Apply two coats of exterior paint.

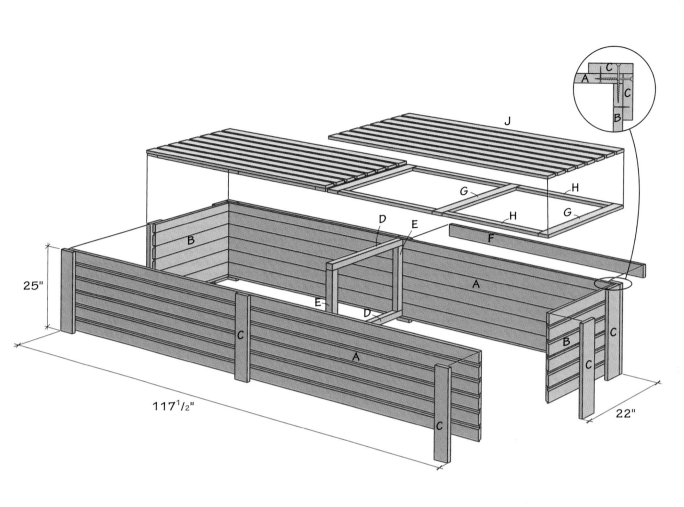

25"

117¹/₂"

22"

A B C D E F G H J

Bench with Bicycle Rack

This bench might be a little odd, but it is hugely appreciated by the girl who owns it.

She lives in a small townhouse with a very narrow sidewalk at the front.

The sidewalk is not wide enough to fit in both a bench and a bicycle.

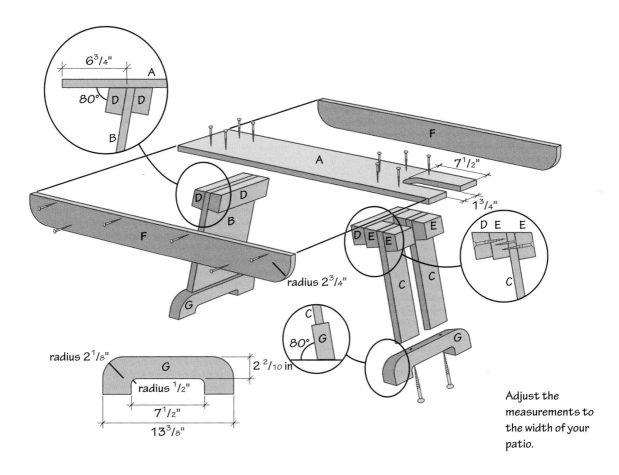

6³/₄"

80°

A

D D

B

F

7¹/₂"

A

1³/₄"

D E E

radius 2³/₄"

D E E

C

C

C

E

C

80° G

G

G

2 ²/₁₀ in

radius 2¹/₈"

G

radius ¹/₂"

7¹/₂"

13³/₈"

Adjust the measurements to the width of your patio.

Materials

Dimensional planed lumber, ⁷/₈ × 7³/₄ inches, approx. 4 feet 11 inches:

    1 piece × 40 inches (A)

    1 piece × 15 inches (B)

Dimensional planed lumber, ⁷/₈ × 3³/₄ inches, approx. 9 feet 10 inches:

    2 pieces × 15 inches (C) cut 3 inches wide

    2 pieces × 40 inches (F)

Supports, 1³/₄ × 2³/₄ inches, approx. 3 feet 3 inches:

    3 pieces × 7³/₄ inches (D)

    4 pieces × 3 inches (E)

Feet, 1³/₄ × 3³/₄ inches, approx. 2 feet 3 inches:

    2 pieces × 13³/₈ inches (G)

Wood glue for outdoor use

Screws

Wood putty

Exterior enamel paint

Since the ground slopes at this home, we cut the feet obliquely so that the bench stands straight.

Here's what you do:

Note: All screw holes should be countersunk and the screws sunk below the surface of the wood.

1. Saw out the slot at one end of the seat board A.

2. Saw the supports D and E at a 10° angle along one of the narrow long edge. Then cut them to suitable lengths.

3. Saw the leg parts B and C at a 10° angle at one end.

4. Glue and screw the outer support D onto the leg B. Glue and screw on the inner support D.

5. Glue and screw together the parts C, E and D. Drill pilot holes into the blocks E, otherwise there is a good chance the screws will split them.

6. Glue and screw seat board A into the leg frame with the planed side up.

7. With a jigsaw, add a 3 inch radius to both ends of the trim pieces F. Glue and screw F into A and E into D.

8. Jigsaw and sand the feet G.

9. Cut the bottom of the feet G at a 10° angle.

10. Drill pilot holes into G. Glue and screw G into B and C, respectively.

11. Cover the screw heads with filler. Sand.

12. Apply two coats of exterior enamel paint.

Table with Benches

We have made lots of benches and tables, both for us and for friends, but always with a rectangular shape. This time I wanted to make a square table, as I feel it is better for social interaction.

I wanted benches with space for two people, so that nobody has to climb over anybody else to get out. The result is excellent and now we are just missing the blue and white striped cushions that I hope to be able to sew before autumn comes.

Square table

Materials

Dimensional planed lumber, $2^3/4 \times 2^3/4$ inches, approx. 11 feet 9 inches:

    4 pieces × 29 inches (A)

    4 pieces × $5^1/2$ inches (C)

Dimensional planed lumber, $1^1/2 \times 2^3/4$ inches, approx. 14 feet 1 inch:

    4 pieces × $40^1/2$ inches (B)

Dimensional planed lumber, $1^1/2 \times 1^1/2$ inches, approx. 12 feet 9 inches:

    4 pieces × $4^3/4$ inches (D)

    3 pieces × $42^1/4$ inches (E)

Dimensional planed lumber, $1^1/2 \times 5^1/2$ inches, approx. 34 feet 5 inches:

    4 pieces × 48 inches (F)

    6 pieces × 37 inches (G)

Wood plugs, $3/8 \times 3/8$ inches: 16 pieces

Galvanized steel angle brackets: 10 pieces

Lag bolts

Screws: $3^1/2$ inches and 2 inches

Wood glue for outdoor use

Here's what you do:
Building the Table

Assemble the two pairs of legs using the legs A and the aprons B. Drill holes for dowels in each part then glue and screw the parts together. B should be inset $1/4$ inch from A. Clamp the parts and leave to dry. In order to glue the table, you will need a pair of long clamps. If you don't have any, you can make them yourself, see the description on the next page.

1. In the same way, glue together the leg assemblies with the other two aprons B.

2. Cut notches on the inside point of parts C so they'll fit around the legs. Drill pilot holes and glue and screw them on the corners according to the drawing. Use a lag bolt to screw into the leg.

3. Screw the D parts onto B using angle brackets.

4. Screw the ends of E onto B, again using angle brackets and then screw the E pieces to the D pieces using screws and glue.

5. Miter the ends of the edge parts F at a 45° angle. Glue and clamp them to the table frame. Screw them on from below through B, D and E.

6. To fasten the corners of the F pieces, drill a hole, approx. $3/8$ inch deep in the corners, with a $3/8$ inch drill. Drive in a screw so that it is recessed in the hole. Glue a $3/8$ inch wood plug into the hole. When the glue has dried, saw off the wood plug and sand flush.

7. Glue the boards G in place, screw them on from below through E.

8. Finish the surface of the table, see p. 98.

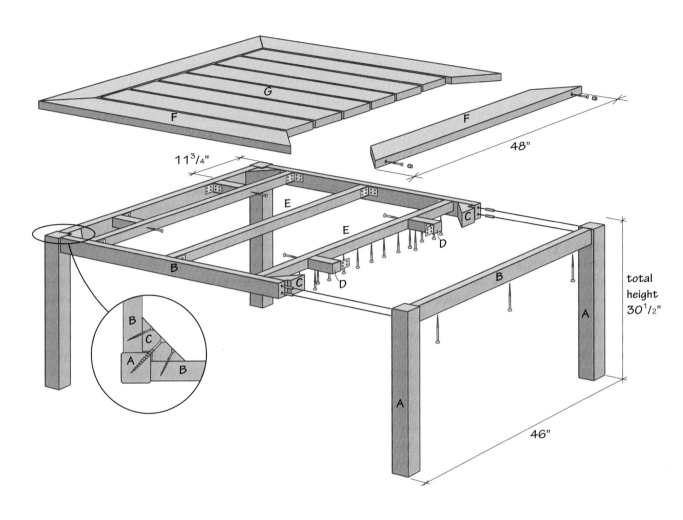

11³/₄"

48"

total height 30¹/₂"

46"

Clamps

Materials

Dimensional lumber, 1¹/₂ × 2¹/₂ inches, approx. 8 feet
2 inches:
    1 piece × 64 inches (H)
    4 pieces × 7 inches (J and K)
Nail plates: 4 pieces
Screws

Here's what you do:

1. Screw on a block J using nail plates at each end of the long stud H.

2. Split two blocks into four wedges (K).

3. Insert the pair of legs consisting of the legs A and the border B. Insert the wedges. Hammer or press together the wedges using clamps.

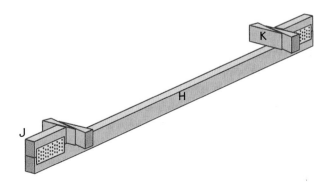

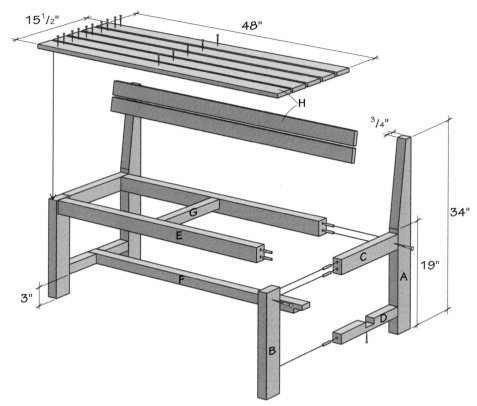

Dimensions shown in figure: 15½", 48", H, ¾", 34", 19", G, E, C, A, F, D, B, 3"

Building the Benches

The description refers to one bench.

Materials

Dimensional planed lumber, $1\frac{1}{2} \times 2\frac{1}{2}$ inches, approx.
18 feet:

 2 pieces × 34 inches (A)
 2 pieces × 18 inches (B)
 2 pieces × 12 inches (C)
 2 pieces × 41 inches (E)

Dimensional planed lumber, $1\frac{1}{2} \times 1\frac{1}{2}$ inches, approx.
70 inches:

 2 pieces × 12 inches (D)
 1 piece × 42 inches (F)

Dimensional planed lumber, $\frac{3}{4} \times 2\frac{1}{2}$ inches, approx. 28 feet
6 inches:

 7 pieces × 48 inches (H)

Wood dowel, $\frac{3}{8} \times 1\frac{1}{2}$ inches: 22 pieces
Screws: 3 inches, $1\frac{5}{8}$ inches
Wood glue for outdoor use

Here's what you do:

1. Saw half-lap joints in both the side stretchers D and the stretcher F.

2. Saw the legs A to achieve a comfortable tilt for the back-rest. Sand the sawed surface.

3. Assemble pairs of legs/side panels from A, B, C and D using wood dowels and glue. Clamp and let the glue dry.

4. Drill holes for dowels at the ends of seat supports E and in B and C and the middle of the long side E.

5. With glue and dowels, assemble the middle crossbar G between the seat supports E. Place a clamp here. Use dowels and glue to assemble the pairs of leg assemblies with both E parts. Use long screws through B and C into E. At the same time glue on F and screw from below through D.

6. Glue and screw on 5 seat boards H. Begin at the back with the board which faces A, then install the front board, which should protrude by $\frac{1}{2}$ inch beyond the front edge of B. Fit the rest of the boards, with even spacing between them.

7. Fit both boards H for the backrest of A. The upper one should protrude $\frac{5}{8}$ inch above A.

8. Finish the surface of the sofa, see p. 98.

How to finish surfaces

Materials
Shellac
Wood sealer
Exterior primer and enamel paint

Here's what you do:
1. Coat all knots with shellac.
2. Apply sealer liberally to the finished pieces (table and benches), especially the bottoms of the legs. Reapply the sealer to keep the wood wet for a short while, then let dry.
3. Apply one coat primer and two coats enamel paint.

Folding Sideboard

Here's a practical and neat spare table that is easy to fold and stow away.
Stenciling text on the table is fun and gives it a personal touch. The text
we chose is perhaps even more suitable for the winter, when the table
can be used as a fruit and vegetable tray in the kitchen.

Materials

Dimensional planed lumber, $3/4 \times 1 1/2$ inches, approx.
19 feet 8 inches:
    4 pieces × 38 inches (A)
    2 pieces × $24 1/2$ inches (B1)
    2 pieces × 23 inches (B2)
Dimensional planed lumber, $1/2 \times 1/2$ inch, approx. 3 feet 3 inches:
    2 pieces × $18 1/2$ inches (C)
Dimensional planed lumber, $1/2 \times 2 1/2$ inches, approx.
21 feet 3 inches:
    6 pieces × $26 1/2$ inches (D)
    2 pieces × $18 1/2$ inches (E)
    2 pieces × $27 1/2$ inches (G)
Dimensional planed lumber, $1/2 \times 1 3/4$ inches:
    1 piece × $27 1/2$ inches (F)
Screws
Wood glue for outdoor use
Machine screw M5 with nut and three washers: 2 pieces
Eye screws: 2 pieces
Chain: approx. 1 foot 3 $3/10$ inches
Wood filler for outdoor use
Shellac
Exterior primer and enamel paint

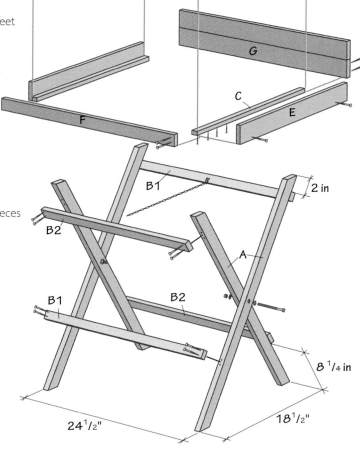

Here's what you do:

Note: All screw holes should be countersunk and the screws sunk below the surface of the wood.

1. Saw the strips A to rough size leaving about one inch extra in length. Drill clearance holes for the machine screws in the middle of the strips. Measure and mark the finished length on A, working out from the middle.

2. Screw the A parts together, making two mirrored pairs. Put the A parts on a flat surface and open them so that the cross formed by the parts is $18 1/2$ inches wide at your length markings. Place a ruler across and mark where the legs should be mitered, then cut them.

3. Fold the leg crosses together and screw and glue on the strips B1 and B2. Make sure all angles are right angles. Drill pilot holes into B1 and B2.

4. Glue and screw together the strips C and the slats D. Drill pilot holes into C and drive screws through C into D. Make sure that the D slats are evenly spaced.

5. Glue and screw on the borders E and then F, holding F flush to the bottom of E.

6. Glue together both boards G for the back panel. Clamp and let the glue dry.

7. Glue and screw the boards G onto E and D.

8. Take the leg frame apart by removing the machine screws in the middle.

9. Cover the screw heads on the tray and leg frame with filler. Sand.

10. Coat all knots with shellac.

11. Paint with primer, let the paint dry and sand lightly.

12. Finish off with two coats of enamel paint.

13. Screw together the leg frame.

14. A chain runs between the legs parts to keep the legs from opening too far. To attach the chain, drive eye screws into the inside of the upper strips B1 and B2, respectively.

15. Unfold the leg frame and place the tray on top.

Gates

Gates should be welcoming and preferably (or so we think) lower in the middle than on the sides. A high gate can seem unfriendly and entice some people to jump over it rather than walk through it. Here we introduce two classic Swedish gates – one is a little more difficult to build than the other, but they both have in common the same message: Welcome, please come inside!

Gate

Materials

Dimensional planed lumber, $1^{1}/_{2} \times 3^{1}/_{2}$ inches, approx.
12 feet:
    2 pieces × 42 inches (A)
    2 pieces × $21^{3}/_{4}$ inches (B)
Dimensional planed lumber, $1^{1}/_{2} \times 5^{1}/_{2}$ inches:
    1 piece × $21^{3}/_{4}$ inches (C)
Lath, $^{1}/_{2} \times 1^{3}/_{4}$ inches, approx. 29 feet 6 inches:
    16 pieces at various lengths (D)
Lath, $^{1}/_{2} \times ^{1}/_{2}$ inches, approx. 4 feet 3 inches:
    6 pieces × $7^{1}/_{4}$ inches (E)
Dowel rod, @ $^{1}/_{2}$ inch diameter – one 36 inch length
required:
Wood dowel, $^{1}/_{2} \times 1^{1}/_{2}$ inches:
12 pieces
Screws and brads
Wood glue for outdoor use
Hook and band hinges: 2 pieces
Gate lock

Here's what you do:

1. Draw a square 1 foot 9 inches
× 1 foot 9 inches on Masonite board. Place one layer of the
lath strips D at a 45° angle against the square. There should be
a $1^{3}/_{4}$ inch gap, put in spacers. Place the next layer in the
same manner, but at a 90° angle. All the parts should protrude
beyond the square on the Masonite board.

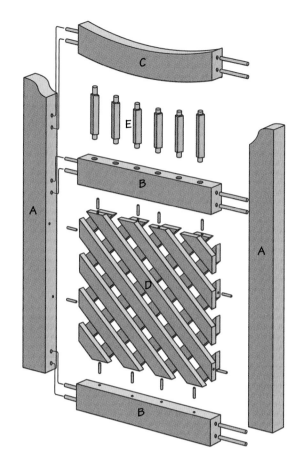

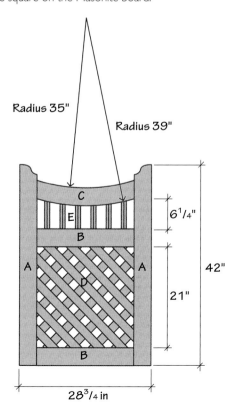

Radius 35"

Radius 39"

$6^{1}/_{4}$"

42"

21"

$28^{3}/_{4}$ in

2. Glue the parts and fix them with a brad in each cross. Make
sure no brads end up outside your square. Let the glue dry.
3. Re-draw the 1 foot 9 inch × 1 foot 9 inch square on the
glued grid and saw along the lines.
4. Draw the curve in part C and saw it with a jigsaw. Sand
a bevel on the edges. Sand bevels on the edges of parts A
and B too.
5. Jigsaw the top of the boards A according to the drawing.
Each square on the drawing represents $^{25}/_{64}$ inch.
6. Drill pilot holes for the slats E at the top of B and C. Place
B and C at the correct distance from each other. Measure
and saw E into suitable lengths. Carve round plugs at the ends
of E with a very sharp knife. Glue together B, C and E.
7. Drill dowel holes for small dowels in the grid D. Using
those holes as a guide, mark and drill dowel holes in both
the crossbars B.
8. Glue together D with both B parts. Clamp and let the
glue dry.
9. Measure and mark very carefully where the large wood
dowels should be at the ends of B and C and in A. Mark
where the small wood plugs should be on the sides of D
and in A. Drill the holes, then glue together all parts. Clamp
and let dry.
10. Finish the surface of the gate, see the next page.
11. Fit the hinges and gate lock.

Double Gate

Materials

Dimensional planed lumber, $1^1/2 \times 3^1/2$ inches, approx.
14 feet:

    2 pieces x 39 inches (A)
    2 pieces x $37^1/2$ inches (B)

Dimensional planed lumber, $3/4 \times 3^1/2$ inches, approx.
18 feet:

    2 pieces x $68^1/2$ inches (C)
    2 pieces x approx. $35^1/2$ inches (D)

Fence pickets, $1/2 \times 1^3/4$ inches, approx. 45 feet 11 inches:

    14 pieces x 39 inches (E)

Screws

Wood glue for outdoor use

Hook and band hinges: 4 pieces

Gate latch

Bolt for gates

Here's what you do:

The gates should be built as one unit and split into two gates
once completed.

1. Saw and chisel dados in posts A and B for the rails C.
2. Place A and B on the floor and insert both rails C. There
should be a $3/8$ inch gap between the two boards B. Glue
and screw together the parts.

3. Place the diagonal braces D in the correct position.
Draw on D where they should be mitered. D should fit
tightly in place. Miter the D parts.
4. Apply glue to the ends and insert pieces D against
pieces A, B and C. Let the glue dry.
5. Glue and screw on the pickets E. Leave E a little long for
now.
6. Draw a line on E from A to B. Saw following the line.
7. Prop up the gate in its place and fit the hinges.
8. Saw through the gate, through both C pieces, between
the B parts.
9. Finish the surface of the gate, see below.
10. Fit a gate latch between the gates and a bolt against the
ground on one of the gates.

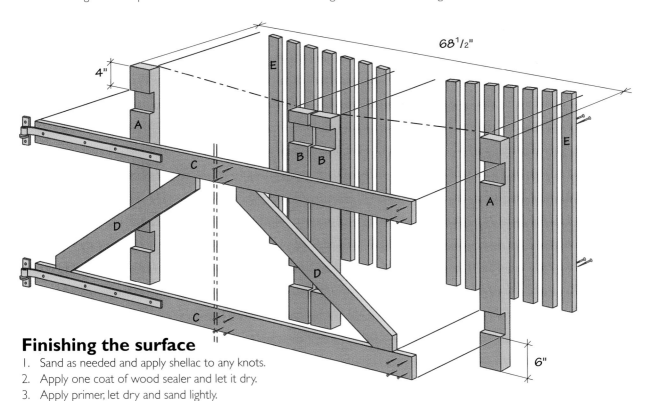

Finishing the surface

1. Sand as needed and apply shellac to any knots.
2. Apply one coat of wood sealer and let it dry.
3. Apply primer, let dry and sand lightly.
4. Apply two coats of exterior enamel paint.

Votives

These large, wonderful votives are made of wood and glass with a vented lid and handle made of bent iron. They make fine indoor or outdoor furnishing details. We put the votives on the entrance stairs in the snow when we have guests for Christmas or New Year's dinner. A good tip is to buy large, and expensive candles. In the long run it is less expensive and they do not drip.

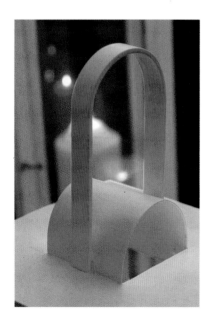

Materials for the small votive

Plywood, $^1/_2$ inch:
  2 pieces × 9 × 9 inches (A)
  4 pieces × 1$^1/_2$ × 1$^1/_2$ inches (C)
Dimensional planed lumber, $^3/_4$ × $^3/_4$ inch, approx. 9 feet 10 inches:
  8 pieces × 5$^1/_2$ inches (B)
  4 pieces × 17$^1/_4$ inches (D)
Trim strip, $^1/_2$ × $^1/_2$ inch, approx. 4 feet:
  2 pieces × 15$^3/_4$ inches (E)
  2 pieces × 5$^1/_2$ inches (F)
Thin sheet steel:
  1 piece × 3$^1/_4$ × 6$^1/_2$ inches (G)
  1 round, @ 3 inch diameter (H)
Steel flat bar, $^1/_8$ × $^3/_4$ inch:
  1 piece × 16$^3/_4$ inches (J)
Glass sheets, $^1/_8$ inch:
  3 pieces × 6 × 16$^1/_8$ inches
  1 piece × 4$^7/_8$ × 15$^1/_8$ inches

Materials for the large votive

Plywood, $^1/_2$ inch:
  2 pieces × 10$^1/_2$ × 10$^1/_2$ inches (A)
  4 pieces × 1$^1/_2$ × 1$^1/_2$ inches (C)
Dimensional planed lumber, $^3/_4$ × $^3/_4$ inch, approx. 13 feet 9 inches:
  8 pieces × 7$^1/_4$ inches (B)
  4 pieces × 28$^1/_4$ inches (D)
Trim strip, $^1/_2$ × $^1/_2$ inch, approx. 5 feet 6 inches:
  2 pieces × 26 inches (E)
  2 pieces × 7$^1/_8$ inches (F)
Thin sheet steel:
  1 piece × 4 × 8 inches (G)
  1 round, @ 3$^1/_4$ inches diameter (H)
Steel flat bar, $^1/_8$ × $^3/_4$ inch:
  1 piece × 2 feet (J)
Glass sheets, $^1/_8$ inch:
  3 pieces × 7$^5/_8$ × 28$^5/_8$ inches
  1 piece × 6$^1/_2$ × 25$^3/_8$ inches

Materials for both

Wood glue for outdoor use
Screws of various dimensions
Small wire nails
Hinges: 2 pieces
Latch
Exterior paint

The drawing shows the smaller votive. The instructions are the same for both votives.

Here's what you do:

1. Begin by sawing $^1/_4$-inch-deep grooves in the strips B and D with a $^1/_4$-inch saw blade in your table saw. Measure and saw the strips before cutting them to length. Cut as follows:
    One track in B2 and D1.
    Two tracks in D2.
    B1 should not have any track.
    Cut the strips at the correct lengths.
2. Draw diagonals on the bottoms of A1 and the lid A2. Mark where the hole in A2 should be. The small cutouts for the handle J should be $^3/_4$ × $^3/_{16}$ inch. Cut out the hole using a jigsaw.
3. Mark exactly where the strips B should be, the diagonals are helpful for this purpose.
4. Glue and nail the strips B2 into A1 and A2. Use a countersink to start the holes in the grooves in B2.
5. Drill pilot holes for the corner posts D1 and D2 in A1.
6. Saw off one corner on each foot C.
7. Glue and screw on the C parts so that they protrude $^3/_{16}$ inch outside A1. Recess the screws.
8. Fix the plate H with one small nail.
9. Screw the corner strips D1 and D2 onto A1. Do not use any glue – that way, if any glass breaks in the future it will be possible to replace it.
10. Bend the steel flat bar to form the handle J. It is hard to

bend it at exactly in the middle, so use a bar that is slightly longer than you need, and cut it afterwards.

11. Drill pilot holes at the ends of the handle J and screw it onto A2.

12. Bend the protective plate G.

13. Drill pilot holes into G and screw the plate onto A2.

14. Drill pilot holes in the lid A2 to drive the screws into the corner strips D1 and D2. Recess the screws.

15. Saw a groove in the strips E and F for the glass sheet of the door.

16. Use a miter saw to saw a 45° angle on the ends of E and F. Glue and nail together the frame for the door.

17. Paint all the parts with your preferred color.

18. Insert the glass sheet between the corner strips D.

19. Cover with the lid A2, glue and screw it in place.

20. Insert a glass sheet in the frame E-F and fix it with small nails or glazer points.

21. Attach the hinges to the door and votive frame and fit the latch.

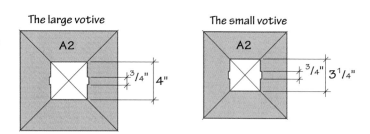

The large votive

A2

³/4" 4"

The small votive

A2

³/4" 3¹/4"

All measurements in feet and inches.

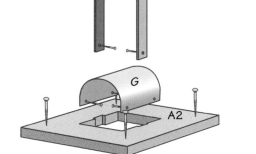

J

G

A2

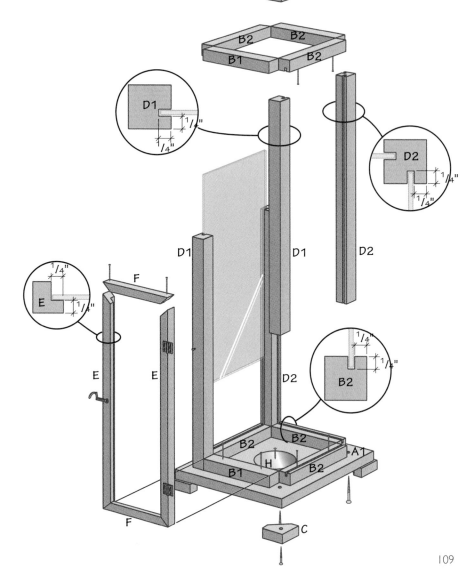

B2 B2

B1 B2

D1

¹/4"

¹/4"

D2

¹/4"

¹/4"

D1 D1 D2

F

¹/4"

E ¹/4"

E E

D2

¹/4"

¹/4"

B2

B2 B2

B1 H B2

A1

F

C

Café Table

We call it a café table because it was inspired by rows of tables in a café in Paris. The rustic and typically southern European touch makes you feel like cutting cheese and salami directly on the table top. The silver-gray surface will become more beautiful as time goes by.

Materials

Dimensional planed lumber, $1\frac{1}{2} \times 7\frac{1}{2}$ inches, approx.
9 feet:

      4 pieces × 24 inches (A)

Dimensional planed lumber, $1\frac{1}{2} \times 2\frac{1}{2}$ inches, approx.
20 feet:

      4 pieces × 26 inches (B)
      4 piece × 16 inches (C)
      2 pieces × 18 inches (D)
      1 piece × 22 inches (E)

Dowel rod, $\frac{1}{2} \times 3\frac{3}{4}$ inches – bought in 36" lengths
Wood dowels, $\frac{3}{8} \times 1\frac{1}{2}$ inches: 24 pieces
Screws, #8 × 3 inches: 20 pieces
Wood glue for outdoor use
Iron sulfate
Water-based stain, silver gray

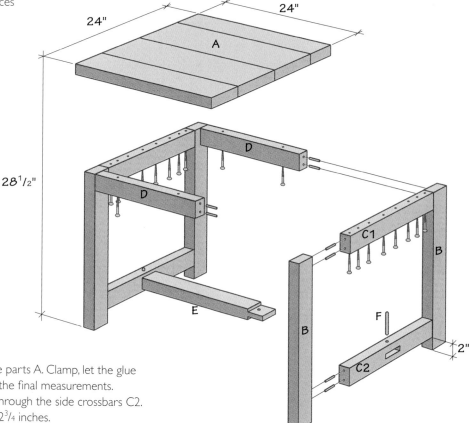

Here's what you do:

1. Saw and glue together the parts A. Clamp, let the glue dry and saw the table top to the final measurements.
2. Drill and chisel mortises through the side crossbars C2. The mortises should be $\frac{1}{2} \times 2\frac{3}{4}$ inches.
3. Saw tenons at both ends of the middle crossbar E. The tenons should be 2 inches. E, excluding the tenons, should have the same length as the rails D. Check that the tenons fit into C2.
4. Drill dowel holes for dowels in the legs B, the rail C1 and the side stretcher C2. Glue together the two pairs of legs. Measure to confirm the diagonals are of equal length, to check that the assemblies are square. Clamp and let the glue dry.
5. Drill dowel holes for dowels in B and D. Glue together the frame. The middle stretcher E should be glued and assembled at the same time. Check the diagonals, clamp the assembly and let the glue dry.
6. Sand the dowel rod F round at both ends. Drill right through C2 and the tenon on E with a $\frac{1}{2}$ inch drill. Apply glue to F tap it into the hole.

7. Place the top upside down, apply glue to the top of the frame and position it on the top. Attach the top by driving screws through C1 and D.
8. Sand and round off all corners on the table.
9. The table can obviously be painted in the usual way. We chose to make a iron sulfate (copperas) solution to give the table a worn look right from the start: Mix $1\frac{3}{4}$ ounces iron sulfate and 0.07 fluid ounces silver gray stain with 35 ounces of warm water. Apply the solution to the table. To start with it will look a little green, but let the table stand outside and be patient, and after a while it will become a beautiful gray.

Stackable Boxes

Having fancy wooden boxes at hand when pulling up carrots or picking apples makes the job more pleasant. These are also stackable so that you can fit a lot in a small space. Apples can be stored in the airy boxes over the winter.

Materials (for one box)

Dimensional planed lumber, $^3/_4 \times 3^1/_2$ inches, approx.
12 inches:
  2 pieces × 20 inches (A)
  2 pieces × 14 inches (B)
Planed strip, $^3/_4 \times {}^3/_4$ inches, approx. 4 feet:
  4 pieces × $8^1/_4$ inches (C)
Strips, $^1/_2 \times 2$ inches, approx. 12 feet:
  8 pieces × $15^1/_2$ inches (D)
Strips, $^3/_4 \times 1^1/_2$ inches, approx. 5 feet:
  2 pieces × 5 inches (E)
  1 piece × $21^1/_2$ inches (F)
  1 piece × 20 inches (G)
Screws
Brads
Wood glue for outdoor use
Exterior paint or stain

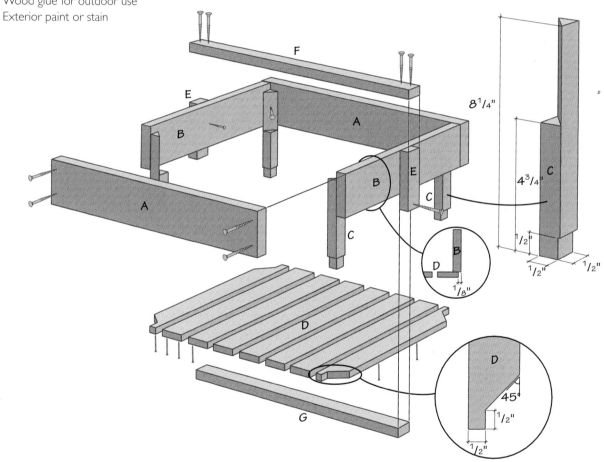

Here's what you do:

1. Glue and screw together parts A and B. Drill pilot holes in A
2. Saw the legs C according to the drawing.
3. Saw the two outer bottom boards D according to the drawing so they fit around the legs and rest on the small shelf formed on the legs. Glue and nail the two outer D parts to the underside of A. Make sure that C can be inserted. Note that the outer slats D do not reach all the way to the edge of B.

4. Glue and screw the four legs C to B.
5. Glue and nail the other bottom boards D to A, evenly spacing them.
6. Glue and screw the strips E to B. Then glue and screw F to the ends of E and finally G to E.
7. Apply one coat of paint or stain.

Planting Table or Outdoor Kitchen

When you have spent a lot of time building projects, it is nice to be able to use them in several different ways. Our solid planting table, with a top made of galvanized sheet metal, can be transformed into a kitchen. This is appreciated both by us and by guests because it means we can chat while the food is being prepared. Or, as we often do, let the guests help – a great way to socialize!

Materials

Dimensional planed lumber, 1 1/2 × 1 1/2 inches, approx.
66 feet:

- 4 pieces × 48 inches (A)
- 6 pieces × 24 inches (B)
- 2 pieces × 36 inches (C)
- 2 pieces × 57 inches (D)
- 4 pieces × approx. 34 inches (E)
- 2 pieces × approx. 55 inches (F)

Rough-cut board, 3/4 × 3 1/2 inches, approx. 104 feet:

- 8 pieces × 48 inches (G)
- 5 pieces × 52 inches (H)
- 7 pieces × 52 inches (J)
- 3 pieces × 54 inches (O)
- 2 pieces × 25 inches (P)

Dimensional planed lumber, 1/2 × 3 1/2 inches, approx. 5 feet:

- 2 pieces × 2 feet 3 inches (K)

Furring strips, 3/4 × 1 1/2 inches, approx. 6 feet:

- 2 pieces × 6 3/4 inches (L)
- 2 pieces × approx. 7 1/2 inches (M)
- 2 pieces × 6 inches (N)
- 2 pieces × 4 3/4 inches (L1)
- 2 pieces × approx. 4 3/8 inches (M1)
- 2 pieces × 3 3/4 inches (N1)

Galvanized sheet metal, 1/64 inch thick:

- 27 inches × 57 inches

Galvanized angle brackets: 12 pieces

Sheet metal screws

Wood glue for outdoor use

Screws of various sizes

Exterior paint

Here's what you do:

You will achieve the best results if you have access to a miter saw.

1. Screw together the studs A and B into two frames with a crossbar in the middle. Use angle brackets to reinforce the joints.

2. Attach the legs C and D to the frames with long screws.

3. Measure the exact length and angle of the crosses E by placing them against the legs and marking. Cut the crosses. Mark for half-lap joints where the E parts overlap each other. Saw and chisel out the half-laps. Put the crosses together with glue. put them in the correct position and screw them to the frames. Clamp the half-lap joint until the glue has dried.

4. Repeat with the F parts for the cross on the back.
5. Saw the boards G. The front and the back panels are also sawed lengthwise so that the width of the tongue-and-groove board is 2 feet 2 inches (most easily done with a circular saw). Screw the boards G onto the lower frame.
6. Saw the boards H to length. Screw the boards H onto the upper frame. Note that they should be spaced, to

(M1) and mark how the ends of M (M1) should be mitered. Saw M (M1) then glue M (M1) to L and N (L1 and N1). Clamp and let the glue dry.
10. Glue and screw on the brackets from behind.
11. The O parts should be sawed lengthwise at a suitable width. Attach the shelf O with screws.
12. The front and back O pieces are also sawed lengthwise

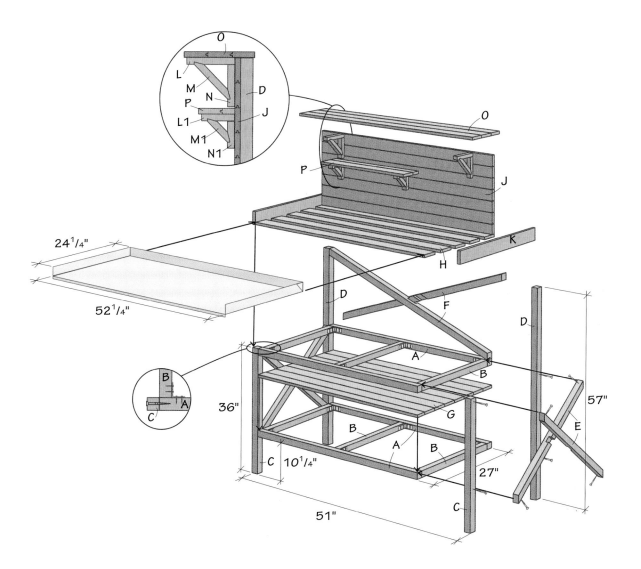

prevent water from collecting between the lumber and the sheet steel.
7. Screw the boards J starting from the bottom and upwards. Saw the last one lengthwise so that it is flush with the upper edge of D.
8. Glue and screw the trim K on both sides. Fasten it to H, J and D but not to B.
9. Glue and screw together the brackets L and N (and L1 and N1). Put diagonal brace M (or M1) across the parts and measure where the notches should be made. Saw the notches in L and N (and L1 and N1). Place these over M

so that the tongue and groove are not visible. Attach the shelf O with screws.
13. Sand and apply putty if needed. Round the front, upper corners of the trim boards K. Coat all knots with shellac. Paint.

It is hard to bend the sheet yourself, but you can order it from a tinsmith or metal shop. Put the sheet in place, it does not need to be held down.

A Little More How-to

While the projects in this book are easily within the scope of any woodworker, we don't want to presume that all our readers are woodworkers. To help those who are new to woodworking, we've included this section that offers additional information on some of the joinery used in the projects. We hope this makes the projects more accessible and more enjoyable.

Creating a Rabbet

A rabbet is a two-sided groove running along one (or more) edges of a board. While usually running with the grain, a rabbet can be run across the grain as well. A rabbet can be created with a router and the appropriate-size/style bit, or with a table saw (as only two of many ways available). The table saw method is shown below. Rabbets are used in the Growing Cabinet, starting on page 8.

STEP ONE: First, set the distance between the fence and blade (in our case we're cutting a $3/8$" rabbet in $1 1/2$" × $1 1/2$" stock, so the setting is for $1 1/8$"). The blade height is then set to $3/8$".

STEP TWO: The first cut is made simply with the corner receiving the rabbet facing down and away from the fence. Remember to use the safety devices provided with your saw. We have the guard removed here to better show the cut.

STEP THREE: Flip the piece end-for-end and then rotate the piece to put the first cut facing down and away from the fence. Make the second cut.

STEP FOUR: The waste piece will fall safely away from the cut, and your rabbet is complete.

Creating a Cross-lap

Cross-lap joints are mating cuts across the grain on two pieces. The cuts are the same in each part, removing the width of the other part and cutting half the depth of the piece. When the two halves are assembled this joint provides good gluing surface and provides strength against racking. This joint can be created with hand tools, on a table saw, or with a jigsaw, as shown here. Cross-laps are used in the Long Bench (starting on page 14), and in the Awning on page 34.

STEP ONE: For the Long Bench we are using $1\frac{1}{2}$" × $1\frac{1}{2}$" stock. It's easiest to use the pieces themselves to lay out the joint. Locate the position and use the mating piece to mark the width.

STEP TWO: Determine the depth of the joint (half the thickness of the piece), in this case $\frac{3}{4}$", and mark that depth on one side of the piece.

Creating a Cross-lap (cont.)

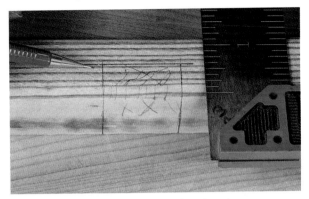

STEP THREE: Connect your lines and continue the same lines around the piece to the other side. Mark out the area to be removed to avoid any mistakes.

STEP FOUR: Most jigsaws offer different cutting settings. The most aggressive setting causes the blade to move forward in the cut. In this case we don't want that so change your setting to "0".

STEP FIVE: Make two cuts into the piece to define the width of the joint. You want to cut to the inside of the lines (in the waste area) to make sure that you leave the lines defining the width. If you're not familiar with using a jigsaw this may take a little practice. If you're unsure, cut further from the line then use a chisel to pare away the waste until you reach your marks.

STEP SIX: With the two sides defined, the next cut is a sweeping cut from the top of one joint edge to the bottom of the other. You want to reach the bottom line somewhere near the middle to create a flat cut leading to the bottom of the other side wall cut. Go slow with the turn as jigsaws can buck if turned too quickly in a cut.

STEP SEVEN: With the first waste section out of the way (shown still in the shot here for perspective), start your second cut on the flat at the bottom of the half lap and saw back toward the left side of the joint. As the piece falls away your cross lap is complete on this piece. You may need to do a little bit of clean-up with a chisel or file.

STEP EIGHT: The mating cut in the second piece is just like the first. You can easily define the location and size of the second cut by using the first cut. When both halves are created a little bit of fitting may be required (using a chisel or file) to make the joint fit together perfectly.

Creating a Flat Cross-lap

In some instances a cross-lap joint can be used to join two wide boards as shown at left, and as used in the Woodshed on page 16. The cross lap is a particularly useful joint in this instance because it's a strong joint that also keeps the finished assembly from appearing to be too bulky. By using a cross lap, the finished depth is no greater than a single board. While the previous cross lap was created with a jigsaw, a flat cross-lap is best created on a table saw. You can use a single blade to create the joint, or to speed things up a dado stack can be used. We've shown the single blade option here.

STEP ONE: Start by determining the position and angle where the two boards will meet. The angle may not be critical, but the point where the boards attach to the structure will be. Cut the boards to length only after the center joint is complete. Mark the width on the top board and draw lines lines across the bottom board.

STEP TWO: Mark the depth (half the thickness of the board) on the edge of the pieces. Remember to mark out the waste sections to avoid mistakes. You can choose to connect the lines or not. You won't need to be following the depth lines as the table saw setting will do most of that work.

STEP THREE: Using your half-thickness mark as a guide, run the saw blade up to the proper height. Make sure you're using the tallest tooth on the blade to determine when the blade meets the line.

STEP FOUR: We're using the miter gauge to control the angle of the cut. Get as close to the correct angle setting as possible and make your first cut to the inside of the line, removing only material from the waste area.

Creating a Flat Cross-lap (cont.)

STEP FIVE: After your first cut, flip the piece over to check your angle. As you can see here, a half-degree off on the miter gauge can shift your cut. As we've left the boards long at this point, the perfect angle isn't necessary, but they side wall cuts of the joint will need to be parallel.

STEP SIX: Before making the second cut, use the mating board to double check the second cut's location. Lay the board against the edge of the saw kerf and mark the second line. Carry that line to the edge of the board, then complete the second cut. Remove the waste by continuing to run the board over the blade, advancing a fraction of an inch each time.

STEP SEVEN: After making a few overlapping cuts with the single saw blade, I decided to check my cut. As you can see here, my depth wasn't as deep as I wanted it to be. I slowly raised the blade making deeper cuts until I achieved the proper depth (at the right of the cut). I then re-cut the rest of the section to even up the depth. Best to find out early in the process.

STEP EIGHT: With the cut complete very little clean-up is required. Go ahead and cut the mating piece before doing any clean up with a chisel. The rough left by the saw blade cuts provides a nice fine fit adjustment for the depth of the joint by lightly planing down the high spots left by the saw cuts.

Creating a Half-lap

A half-lap joint is essentially a cross lap that has one side. Half-lap joints can meet at a corner, or a half lap can mate with a cross lap to intersect a longer piece (as shown here). Making the joint is similar to the process used with the cross lap. We've used a table saw and the same process used with the flat cross-lap joint to give an alternative approach to this joint. The half-lap we're creating here is used in the Long Bench on page 14 and also in the Garden Bench on page 32. A note on safety - it's not possible to make these cuts with a guard in place, so be very conscious of the exposed blade.

STEP ONE: First, lay out the joint using the same technique as before. Then, create the cross lap in the mating piece. On the table saw, it's the same as the jigsaw. First define the two sides of the joint, then nibble away the waste between the two cuts.

STEP TWO: Bring the mating piece to the piece with the cross-lap cut and use the joint to locate and mark the position of the half-lap. You need to know the width of the cut, but the depth is already set with the blade height on the table saw.

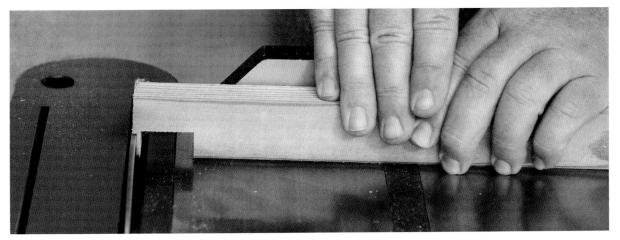

STEP THREE: Define the shoulder of the joint first and then nibble away the waste, starting at the shoulder and workout out to the end of the piece. You may find that your overlap cuts don't always always overlap, leaving a loose "tooth." Don't worry, just make another pass at that location and all will be well.

Creating Radius Cuts

Both concave and convex cuts can be easily created on a board using either a bandsaw or jigsaw. We're showing the method using a jigsaw to create the curves used in the Planting Table on page 20. The bandsaw offers a more reliable vertical edge as a jigsaw's blade can flex during a cut, but the less-expensive jigsaw can also get the work done. Unlike when cutting the cross-lap joint, a more aggressive cut on the jigsaw will help keep the edge square. Set the cut to medium. Whether concave or convex, the cut is the same. You may notice that your jigsaw tends to "pull" to the left or right, making tracking to a line difficult. Remember as you switch directions in the cut that the "pull" may be different. Always leave a little extra material outside the line to clean up.

STEP ONE: Laying out the curves is easiest using a compass. The piece we're working on used two different radii settings on the same piece. Set for the larger radius first using your preferred measuring instrument.

STEP TWO: With the radius set, place the pencil at the bottom corner (upside down here) of the piece and let the stationary leg of the compass rest on the bottom edge.

STEP THREE: Swing the pencil up to the top of the arc and stop there. That's the first curve.

STEP FOUR: I've gone ahead and used the Planting Table as the sample here and continued the straight line from the top of the first curve to the location of the next. Here I'm resetting the compass to match the piece.

STEP FIVE: With the compass reset, move the pencil leg to the top of the board (upside down here) and place the stationary leg on the "top" edge. Then swing the pencil leg down to complete the curve.

STEP SIX: Now to cutting. When cutting curves it's often useful to make clearance cuts at intervals along the pattern. Now when you're cutting the critical curves, your waste piece(s) won't hang loose or interfere with your progress but simply fall away.

STEP SEVEN: Starting from the botom of the pattern, I cut along the convex curve, staying slightly wide of the line on the waste side. The first cut stops when the waste piece is free.

STEP EIGHT: The process continues along the straight length of the shape.

STEP NINE: With the concave curve complete and the last waste piece freed, the piece is nearly done.

STEP TEN: No matter how good the cut, you'll likely need to clean up the edge with a file or rasp.

Creating Multiple Pieces

Sometimes a project requires a lot of pieces that are exactly the same. With larger pieces the concept is simple, but when working with smaller pieces, safety becomes more critical. The small dividers in the Sun Bed's frame on page 66 are a good example. One method to safely cut the many similar pieces is with a miter saw and a stop. We also want to show a simple way to do this task safely on a table saw. A guard should be used to create these cuts, but we have removed it for visual clarity.

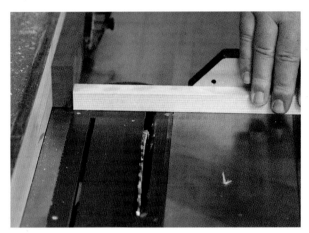

STEP ONE: A general rule is to never use a miter gauge and the rip fence on a table saw at the same time. The danger is trapping a piece between the blade and the fence and causing a dangerous kickback. That's why we use a step-off block clamped to the fence so the block ends an inch or so before your workpiece will contrct the saw blade. Using the step-off block lets you gauge the proper length for the cut against the block. The size of the block isn't critical, just make sure you add that dimension to your final length of your pieces.

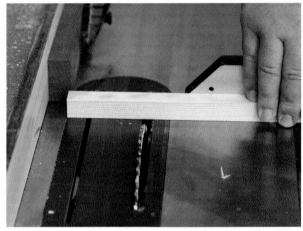

STEP TWO: With the length set, tightly grip the piece against the miter gauge and move the gauge forward. Your piece clears the block before entering the cut, avoiding any concern of kickback.

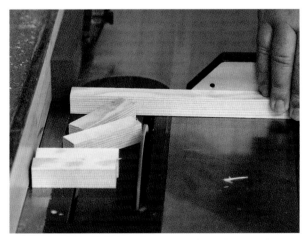

STEP THREE: It isn't my usual method to leave pieces on the saw like this, but you can see that as the blocks turn in the space, they don't kick back. it's also safer than trying to remove small pieces near a running blade.

STEP FOUR: As mentioned earlier, a miter saw also works well. One option is to make a mark on the fence to set your length, but the more accurate version is to clamp a stop block to the fence.

Creating a Long Taper

Ripping a piece of wood to width isn't too difficult, but when faced with a tapering width, there is a little challenge. The angles possible with most miter gauges or sleds on a table saw can't handle as tight an angle as needed for the taper required for the benches in the Table with Benches project on page 92. A circular saw is a possibility, as is a hand saw, but a band-saw or jigsaw offers more speed and control. The technique for either tool is esssentially the same, but we've shown the jigsaw option in these photos.

STEP ONE: The first step is to determine the location of the taper. You need to mark where the taper will end midway down the back pieces (above at right) and how far from the back edge of the leg the cut will be offset (above at left). With those two points determined it's simply connect the dots. A straight edge is the perfect tool, but in a pinch the factory edge of a piece of plywood (above) will do nicely. Go ahead and shade the waste section to avoid confusion.

STEP TWO: (Right) Cut along your line, keeping the blade to the waste side of the cut. Cut as close as you can to reduce cleanup.

STEP THREE: Clean up the cut edge with a bench plane or block plane, as shown here.

Creating a Through Mortise-and-Tenon

The Cafe Table on page 110 uses a through mortise-and-tenon joint to attach a lower stretcher to the to leg assemblies. This joint is more complicated than those we've looked at so far, but is still easily accomplished using a table saw, drill (or drill press) and mallet and chisel.

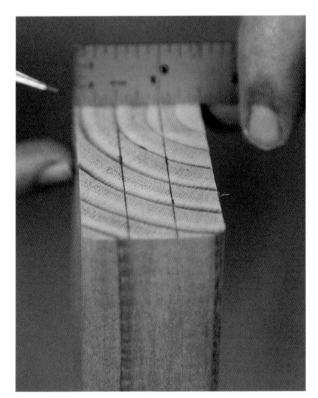

STEP ONE: A running discussion in woodworking is whether to create the mortise or tenon first. In this case I start with the tenon, but you could just as easily start with the mortise. The first step is to lay out the tenon, starting with the thickness. A general rule is that a tenon should be 1/3 the thickness of the piece. In this case that requires a tenon 1/2" thick.

STEP TWO: To lay out the rest of the tenon's shape, you need to know the length of the tenon. As this is a through tenon, it should project beyond the mortise. For our purposes we've taken the thickness of the mortised piece (1 1/2") and added another 1/2", giving us a tenon length of 2".

STEP THREE: With the tenon location defined, head to the table saw. I'm using a miter gauge, and I have the fence set 2" from the blade (our tenon length). I thought I had the blade height set for $1/2$". As the cut on the right shows, the blade was too high. I reset the height until it was just right (the cut on the left).

STEP FOUR: Just as with the half-lap, nibble the rest of the waste material from the one side of the tenon. You can see my slightly-deeper first cut at the top of the tenon. Conveniently this will be hidden by the mortise once the joint is assembled.

STEP FIVE: To complete the tenon, flip the piece over and continue to nibble away. We're essentially creating to half-lap joints to create a tenon.

STEP SIX: With the tenon complete, we have crisp edges and a little bit of tooth on the tenon surface for fine adjustment, once the mortise is complete. If this tenon had been shouldered (the width thinner than the width of the board), we would have run the sides of the board past the blade using the same table saw setup, creating a $1/2$" shoulder all the way around the tenon.

Creating a Through Mortise-and-Tenon (cont.)

STEP SEVEN: Why measure when you have the actual piece to fit? Use the finished tenon to lay out the mortise location in the stretcher. You will work from center lines (both height and width) on the stretcher.

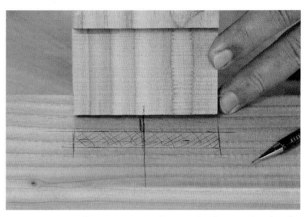

STEP EIGHT: Once the location lines are in place, go ahead and finish drawing the shape of the mortise on the stretcher.

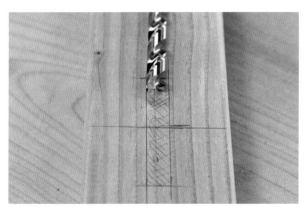

STEP NINE: While you can create a mortise with just a chisel and mallet, you can remove much of the waste by first drilling it out. A $\frac{1}{2}$" bit fits just fine for this joint.

STEP TEN: I used a hand-held drill to remove the waste. Be sure to keep the drill perpendicular to the face of the piece to keep the walls of the mortise square. Overlapping holes reduces the amount of waste to clean up.

STEP ELEVEN: Now all that's needed is to square up the mortise. I'm using an engineer's square to help keep my first cut perpendicular at the end of the mortise.

STEP TWELVE: The walls are next. As you get closer to size, check the fit of your tenon. Because this is a through mortise, the mortise shape will be visible, so make sure the mortise walls are parallel, then fit the tenon.

Creating a Dowel Joint

Dowel joints will never replace a mortise-and-tenon joint for strength, but the convenience and short learning curve are attractive. Dowel joints are used in the benches in the Table with Benches project on page 92. The benches are made from dimensional 2x4 material, and because of that we'll start by looking at a common doweling jig set (shown at right). Most dowelling sets include a clamp-on guide, and three sets of guide collar, stop collar and drill bit (largest and smallest are shown here.

STEP ONE: When working with $^3/_4$"-thick material, the center location on the guide centers the guide collar. For thicker, or thinner material one of the other two locations will locate the center.

STEP TWO: The stop collar is used to control the depth of the hole made by the drill bit. This depth should normally be slightly deeper than half the length of the dowel. You will need to consider the length of the guide collar and the jig itself to make sure your hole is deep enough.

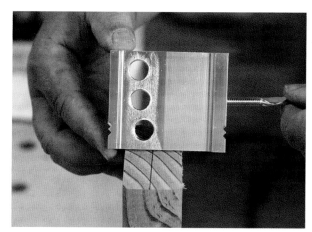

STEP THREE: Unfortunately we're working with 2x4s in this project, and our doweling jig won't locate center in that thick a board. So we'll have to be a bit more creative.

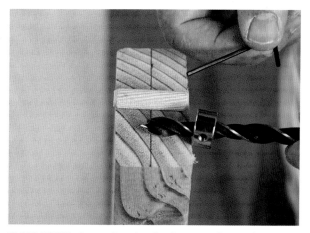

STEP FOUR: As mentioned earlier, the stop collar attaches to the drill bit to control the depth of cut. This isn't a perfect science as the Allen screw in the collar doesn't always clamp onto the bit at a convenient location. In fact, it may be impossible to mount it perpendicular to the bit and can damage the cutting flutes.

Creating a Dowel Joint (cont.)

STEP FIVE: As an option to the stop collar, you can wrap a piece of tape to the drill bit to indicate the desired depth of the hole. Be careful if using the method as there is not physical stop when drilling, only your hand-eye coordination.

STEP SIX: When working freehand to drill dowel holes, you are also missing the guidance of the collar and jig that holds the bit perpendicular to the workpiece. While not absolutely critical, it's still a good idea to have the dowels square to the end. Drill carefully and check your bit's orientation to the surface.

STEP SEVEN: With your dowel holes drilled, double check the fit of the dowels. They should be snug and require a light tap to seat them in the holes.

STEP EIGHT: To locate the mating spot for the dowels we use a set of dowel centers. These are usually included with the dowelling jig and coordinate in size (two of each) for the small, medium and large bit sizes. The centers are simply slipped into the existing holes...

STEP NINE: ...and then the board is placed over the other location and tapped with a hammer or mallet. I lifted the board, but left the dowel centers in position.

STEP TEN: Next, simply move the dowel centers out of the way and drill at the dimpled locations left by the dowel centers.

STEP ELEVEN: To make the joint add some glue to the holes in the piece, then tap the dowels into place until the bottom out in each of the holes.

STEP TWELVE: Add some more glue to the complimentary holes in the other piece (and a little glue on the two surfaces won't hurt), then slide the dowels home. A couple of taps with a hammer to seat the two pieces, and then a clamp and some drying time for the glue.

STEP THIRTEEN: No fancy dowelling jig? No problem. Woodworkers are always creative, and with a few brad nails and an end-cuting plier, you're in business. Simply drive the brad nails part way into the board at the dowel locations.

STEP FOURTEEN: The use the end-cutting pliers to nip the head off the brads, leaving about $^3/_8$" protruding. The pliers leave a clipped end to the nail that is sharp enough for the next step.

STEP FIFTEEN: Position the mating board above the nails and give it a sharp rap with a mallet or hammer. The nails will leave dimples at the dowel locations.

STEP SIXTEEN: Use the end pliers to pull the nails and drill your dowel holes. Simple.

Thank you!

Firstly to our fantastic editor, Roger Carlson, who, with extraordinary calm and patience, has pushed us forward to finish this book. You are always meticulous, competent and reliable. We love your sense of humor, which has made all our conversations pleasant and easygoing. And as we like to say: Work should be fun!

We also want to thank Anna's brother Patrick, who helped us build the large projects in this book, for example the large patio on p. 52 and the fence with trellises on p. 72. It is always a pleasure to spend time and work with you!

Finally, we want to mention our girls Ida and Hilda, simply because they so often have to put up with listening to our chats about project upon project at the dinner table.

Anna and Anders

www.icabokforlag.se

Forma Books AB is a subsidiary of Forma Publishing Group, which is environmentally certified according to SS-EN ISO 14001.

Photos: Anna Jeppsson
Drawings: Anders Jeppsson
Graphic design: Anna and Anders Jeppsson
Editor: Roger Carlson
Printed: 2014

ISBN 978-91-7401-333-7

www.icabokforlag.se

Ideas. Instruction. Inspiration.

These and other great *Popular Woodworking* products are available at your local bookstore, woodworking store or online supplier.

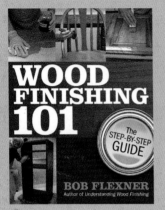

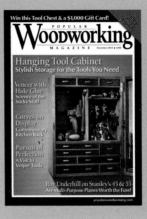

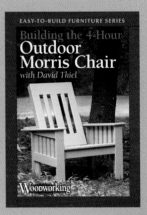

WOOD FINISHING 101
By Bob Flexner

Wood finishing doesn't have to be complicated or confusing. Wood Finishing 101 boils it down to simple step-by-step instructions and pictures on how to finish common woods using widely-available finishing materials. Bob Flexner has been writing about and teaching wood finishing for over 20 years.

paperback • 128 pages

I CAN DO THAT! WOODWORKING PROJECTS

This book will show you how to build 38 quality furniture projects that can be completed by any woodworker using basic tools and materials available at any home center. See how to perform the basic operations in a step-by-step format and build real furniture.

paperback • 176 pages

POPULAR WOODWORKING MAGAZINE

Whether learning a new hobby or perfecting your craft, *Popular Woodworking Magazine* has expert information to teach the skill, not just the project. Find the latest issue on newsstands, or you can order online at popularwoodworking.com.

SHOPCLASS VIDEOS

Learn to build a simple, stylish outdoor chair in four hours or less and with $80 worth of home center materials. Step-by-step instructions for a Morris chair with adjustable back. Create a superb outdoor chair for less money and less time than you can imagine.

Available at shopwoodworking.com
DVD & Instant download

POPULAR WOODWORKING'S VIP PROGRAM
Get the Most Out of Woodworking!

Join the Woodworker's Bookshop VIP program today for the tools you need to advance your woodworking abilities. Your one-year paid renewal membership includes:

Popular Woodworking Magazine (1 year/7 issue U.S. subscription — A $21.97 Value)

Popular Woodworking Magazine CD — Get all issues of **Popular Woodworking Magazine** from 2006 to today on one CD (A $64.95 Value!)

The Best of Shops & Workbenches CD — 62 articles on workbenches, shop furniture, shop organization and the essential jigs and fixtures published in **Popular Woodworking** and

20% Members-Only Savings on 6-Month Subscription for Shop Class OnDemand

10% Members-Only Savings at Shopwoodworking.com

10% Members-Only Savings on FULL PRICE Registration for Woodworking In America Conference (Does Not Work with Early Bird Price)

and more....

Visit *popularwoodworking.com* to see more woodworking information by the experts, learn about our digital subscription and sign up to receive our weekly newsletter at *popularwoodworking.com/newsletters/*

Follow Popular Woodworking